PRAISE FO

MW00913132

"Ran Zilca's *Ride of Your Life* guide is a rare collection of scientifically-sound advice fused with unique spiritual experiences, which is bound to lead you into a transformative journey through life."

—Deepak Chopra

"If you are in need of inspiration to go after your dreams, Ran Zilca's story will deliver. It's an amazing five-week voyage into the depths of Ran's mind from which he bounces up into a new and meaningful future."

—Margaret Moore (aka Coach Meg), MBA, Founder & CEO, Wellcoaches Corporation

"From the stories that my coaching clients share with me, I see how life offers a wealth of outstanding opportunities to those who answer the call of the road. Ran Zilca's story provides a remarkable glance into the internal world of a man who decided to answer the call. His beautiful book will make you laugh, cry, reflect, and awaken your dreams, inspiring you to answer your own call and go on the *Ride of Your Life*."

—Caroline Adams Miller, MAPP, author of *Creating Your Best Life*

"In this enjoyable read you'll befriend Ran Zilca during his soul-searching life transformation and find yourself resonating with his fears, his yearnings, and his well-earned insights. A fresh offering within the positive psychology genre, beguilingly effective for its diary format."

—Barbara L. Fredrickson, Ph.D., author of *Positivity and Love 2.0* and Director of the Positive Emotions and Psychophysiology Lab at UNC-Chapel Hill

"If you are thinking of changing your life, this book will be your loyal companion. Many themes run through Zilca's story: the science of positive psychology, the wisdom of ancient traditions, the power of human connections, and the agency that fuels the process of change. This extraordinary book is both fun to read and deep in its impact, and it will make you rethink your fundamental perspective on life."

—Michelle Gielan, Founder of the Institute for Applied Positive Research and former CBS News anchor

"*Ride of Your Life* is a cross between Gretchen Rubin's *The Happiness Project* and the Dalai Lama's *The Art of Happiness*. Ran Zilca has carved out a whole new literary genre—the positive psychology travel memoir. Some people will read this book for its wisdom and insights, others will read it for the scientist interviews, but regardless of specific interest, anyone who reads this book will be sowing seeds of change, finishing it as a slightly different person than before he/she started."

—Sonja Lyubomirsky, Ph.D., author of *The Myths of Happiness*

"*Ride of Your Life* is a story about each and every one of us who is daring to ask the simple question: "What would happen if I said YES to the journey calling from within?" Ran Zilca's journey reads joyful, painful, insightful, meaningful, and so real. There is authenticity in his words that will surely reflect your own personal challenges. Join Ran for this ride, it could be the *Ride of Your Life*".

—Dr. Itai Ivtzan, author of *Awareness Is Freedom: A course in Psychology and Spirituality*

RIDE OF YOUR LIFE

A COAST-TO-COAST GUIDE
TO FINDING INNER PEACE

by RAN ZILCA

Booktrope Editions
Seattle WA 2014

Copyright 2014 Ran Zilca

This work is licensed under a Creative Commons Attribution-Noncommercial-No Derivative Works 3.0 Unported License.

Attribution — You must attribute the work in the manner specified by the author or licensor (but not in any way that suggests that they endorse you or your use of the work).

Noncommercial — You may not use this work for commercial purposes.

No Derivative Works — You may not alter, transform, or build upon this work.

**Inquiries about additional permissions
should be directed to: info@booktrope.com**

Cover design initial concept by Lauren Amsterdam
Cover design by Shari Ryan

Print ISBN 978-1-62015-589-9
EPUB ISBN 978-1-62015-610-0

Library of Congress Control Number: 2014921154

To Gili, who knows all the teachings
without having to read a single page, and
to all those who dare to dream.

TABLE OF CONTENTS

WHAT I'VE LEARNED
(INSIGHTS FROM THE ROAD):

- Life is best lived in service of others
- The service of others helps you to accomplish your own dreams
- Your dreams matter
- Comfort kills
- Life is best lived in the real world, authentically, even if it's not fun
- People are good
- Fears are exaggerated
- When the hum of the miles eventually disappears, you become one with the road
- America is full of cows, churches, and corn fields
- You can stay in the same small town for 50 years and still be on the *Ride of Your Life*
- You should prepare thoroughly for the road, but forget all of your plans on the first day of the ride
- The single most important thing in life is family, because a family encompasses most of the above

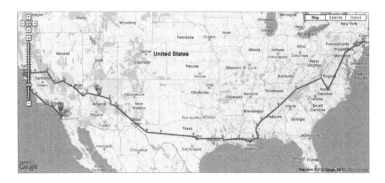

ACKNOWLEDGMENTS

RIDE OF YOUR LIFE BEGAN AS A CONCEPT IN 2009 AND WAS RELEASED in 2014. In the span of these five years, numerous people helped and supported the project in various ways. The person who made this project happen is my wife, Gili, who not only accepted my midlife adventure but also encouraged me to go out and live my childhood dream. My children, Dana, Tomer, and Ori, also embraced their dad's unusual quest, and rooted for me all the way. I am extremely fortunate to have a family that always has my back. The experts interviewed in this book, all of them famous and busy, agreed to meet me on short notice, dedicated their time, and made me feel welcome. I am deeply grateful for the contribution of Phil Zimbardo, Caroline Miller, Barbara Fredrickson, Jamie Pennebaker, Byron Katie, Sonja Lyubomirsky, and Deepak Chopra. A big thanks also goes to Caitlin Eschmann, who stayed in "headquarters" while I was on the road, and to Alison Massie, who has been helping me get the word out about the *Ride* for the past five years. To Roy Denny, the instructor at the Poughkeepsie Motorcycle Safety Course, who taught me how to ride in a way that has probably saved my life more than once. To Lew Goldberg, one of the most prominent psychologists in the past fifty years, whom I am forever indebted to for becoming my friend and my mentor. To Tom Price, who was generous enough to say I "kick ass" even though I was still riding a tiny 250, and let me in the gang; and to his cousin Billy Jessup who gave me his saddle bags and spent an entire day in his garage assembling the speakers on the motorcycle handlebars. Without him, there would have been no soundtrack for this ride.

FOREWORD BY
PHIL ZIMBARDO, PH.D.

WE WOULD ALL LIKE TO THINK THAT WE MAKE DECISIONS AUTONO-
mously, but we never truly do. As uncomfortable as it may be to
accept, we are greatly influenced by social factors like rules, norms,
ideologies, symbols, and language. These factors can prescribe the
way we think, feel, and act, and seduce us to make decisions that
we falsely classify as our own. I started noticing this phenomenon
as a child growing up in the South Bronx, New York City Ghetto,
and continued to study it as a research scientist when I grew up. I
have seen the pervasive and powerful force of situational contexts
on individuals' thoughts, feelings, and behavior in my studies on
cognitive dissonance, cults, dehumanization, evil behavior, and, most
dramatically, in my Stanford Prison Experiment. Beyond any shred
of doubt, situational dynamics can result in major changes in human
behavior, both negative and even positive.

Such influence is not only typical of situations like war and impris-
onment but is also evident in everyday life. The clothes you choose to
wear, the type of car you drive, your nutritional habits, choice of friends,
music favorites, and even your occupation and your romantic mate are
all strongly impacted by social factors. You are constantly subject to
this influence and exposed to it through various channels, although in
recent years, much of it is delivered digitally. Technology has become

the single most powerful knob that can steer human behavior in different directions, including more positive and healthier ones. My former student, friend, and Stanford colleague BJ Fogg was one of the first to identify this tremendous potential of digital technology. Based on his work at the Stanford Persuasive Computing Lab and on the work of many others, new tools have emerged that are designed to change behaviors across many domains, such as healthcare, nutrition, driving habits, addiction, and even promotion of mindful and compassionate behavior. These tools are nothing short of a social-personal revolution. If you examine your own habits and mindsets, it is likely that they have already changed during the past few years thanks to one or more technologies that are installed on your mobile device.

I first met Ran Zilca in the summer of 2009, at the First World Congress on Positive Psychology in Philadelphia. The company he started had developed a pioneering new mobile application that was the first to combine positive psychology interventions into a single self-directed program. Working with top psychologists like Sonja Lyubomirsky, James Pennebaker, and Lew Goldberg, Ran's team had created a range of new digital products that were designed to transform human behavior. Their innovative conceptions laid the cornerstone of what later would become the areas of positive computing and transformative technologies. It was clear to me back then that he is one of the leaders of this exciting revolution and I decided to support the important work his team was doing. A few months later, when he told me about *Ride of Your Life* and asked for an interview, I immediately agreed. Wouldn't you open your front door to someone who has ridden more than five thousand miles on his motorcycle to see you?

At first, I thought that his project was a journalistic attempt to aggregate the work of several scientists and authors from different disciplines. I was wrong. Even though Ran did meet with some of the greatest thought-shapers of our time, his journey was first and foremost a personal one, dealing with some of the most fundamental questions that many of us face about the deeper meaning and purpose in life. As a young man, Ran had followed all the signals, signs, and norms in his environment and was able to excel at his work, be promoted, find a job in a prestigious research lab, and then start a new technology company. Before he reached the age of forty, he was already successful, and by any measure, living the iconic American dream. Yet his success brought with it a sense of restlessness and a feeling that his most intrinsic ambitions and dreams were lost in the process of following the "right" steps, rather than the ideal ones. Just like the "subjects" in my old research studies, he had realized that his choices were not truly his own. In response, he sought an escape out of the Conformity Trap. How? He got a motorcycle license, learned to be an adept biker, started to ride with local bikers, and eventually began planning his coast-to-coast ride. The decision to go on the road was not easy, but his wife was supportive of his quest, and his children were proud of their adventurous father. Eventually, a year after passing the motorcycle road test, he went on the road.

In my research on negative social influence, I found that while most people adhere, there is always a small percentage of people who resist, who rebel, who challenge the situation they are immersed in. I have come to think of those rebels with a cause as *heroes*. They are Everyday Heroes, ordinary people who are willing to risk challenging the status quo regardless of the costs and risks. They question things, defy meaningless or unfair rules, and act in opposition to what they perceive to be unjust.

When Ran and I met in San Francisco and spoke for hours, at first, I was amazed that he seemed even more alert and refreshed than at our earlier meeting—after biking thousands of miles across the American continent. But as we exchanged our ideas and visions,

I realized that he is not only a professional tech pioneer but also a model of an everyday hero. He was, is, a person who refused to accept what his environment had destined him to do and decided to do the unpopular thing. Just like Joseph Campbell's "*Hero with a Thousand Faces*," he answered the call of adventure, faced the risks and challenges of the road, transformed himself, and returned home with the knowledge and powers that he acquired on his journey. Can you follow such a transformation in your life without taking such an enormous trek? Can you challenge the pressures of conformity that are shaping your life in less than the ideal direction for you? I think so, if you are willing to find the source of moral courage inside your being and let it motivate your personal heroic journey. Ran Zilca has decided to share the wealth of his personal experiential knowledge in this fascinating book—that you now hold before you. I invite you to take the first step in your own heroic journey and flip the page. Read on to become the *You* that you were meant to be.

Ride on!

PREFACE

FOUR YEARS AGO, MY LIFE WAS SUPPOSED TO BE PERFECT. ON THE professional front, I was a success story: a veteran of an elite technology unit in the Israeli army, recruited by the world's largest private research lab, then turned hi-tech startup entrepreneur. On the personal front: happily married, three great kids, and a house in the suburbs. On the surface, I was living both the American dream and all that I have personally wished for.

Life was supposed to be perfect, but it wasn't.

Under the surface, daily life was composed of a cautious walk between raindrops of emails, calls, meetings, and carpools. An attempt to stay dry in a torrent of enslaving, often-meaningless obligations. My accomplishments had come at the cost of invisible strings that tied me down. Decisions, big or small, were now dictated by the needs of my career and of my family: work on the weekend, wake up early for Sunday school, buy a house in a good school district, drive a minivan. Life was an infinite conveyer belt of tasks and constraints.

But as hard as it was to be busy, it was scarier to have time to think. In the rare times when I could decide where to go or what to do, I had no idea what I wanted. Yes, I wanted to spend time with my kids and with my wife, but beyond my identity as a husband and father,

I didn't really know who I was anymore. Underneath the layers of being a scientist, a musician, engineer, or businessman, my soul was hiding from me in a silent void.

Like all stories of personal transformation, it all began with a faint nagging ache that gradually grew into a pain. The inevitable feeling that something was seriously missing and had to be retrieved. Nights of reflection turned into weeks, and weeks into months, and at some point, things came to a boil. When they did, a suppressed childhood dream surfaced from the emotional chaos: I want to be a biker. I want to ride the open road, gripping chromed, raised handlebars and stretching forward leather biker boots. I want to ride from coast to coast, through the back roads, with no plans, no reservations, and no schedules. A motorcycle will be my channel to inner peace.

At that time, I had not even sat on a motorcycle before, so some work had to be done. I started pursuing this goal cautiously, one tiny step at a time. First, I took the Motorcycle Safety Course. I spent a weekend in a parking lot in Poughkeepsie trying to operate a motorcycle. I ended up falling down, injuring myself, and flunking the course. Then I went back, passed by a notch, got a tiny 250cc Yamaha, joined a local riding club, and traded it for a bigger motorcycle—a Yamaha V-Star 950. By the late days of spring in the following year, I was ready to go all the way: ride solo from New York to California and mark a big checkmark on my bucket list. My wife, who, in the meantime, had seen her husband transform from a groggy chimp back into a smiling human, supported the endeavor, and the project turned from a dream into a plan. I allocated a modest budget and started preparing to go on the road in the fall.

The plan was to ride alone, from New York to California, and spend all days and nights in solitary contemplation, gathering inspiration from the road and from the people I may meet along the way. It was a simple plan, but it was also a little risky: being away from my family for weeks, with little opportunity to process and discuss my thoughts could possibly be boring, perhaps even depressing. It could be great to take the opportunity to stop along the way and discuss the thoughts that emerge and to process them. Luckily for me, I work with some of the most famous experts whom a person could consult on a soul-searching journey: authors like Deepak Chopra, and prominent psychology researchers like Phil Zimbardo, James Pennebaker, and Sonja Lyubomirsky. I called them and asked if I could stop along the way to chat. They all agreed. *Ride of Your Life* turned from a personal journey into an opportunity to find some broader answers to the questions that people ask as their lives evolve. To marry the wisdom of the road with the professional take of experts, to form a *guide to inner peace*. In preparation for my meetings, I bought two pocket video cameras and two tripods and scheduled approximate dates to see the experts in Maryland, North Carolina, Texas, and California.

On Sunday, September 19, 2010, I took off and headed west, shocked and anxious to leave my family behind, not knowing where I'd be spending the night. In the five weeks that followed, I rode through mountains and valleys, forests and deserts, towns, cities, and oil rigs, in the rain and in sunshine. Six thousand miles later, I got back with answers and had regained my inner peace.

The *Ride* changed forever the lens through which I see the world and affected my life in several different ways: prior to leaving, I met in New York with the founders of a company called bLife. When I reached Los Angeles, I met with them again, ended up selling my company to them, and became bLife's Chief Scientist. I also went on to study life coaching and now actively coach and teach life coaching courses. Two years after I returned, I decided to move with my family to Israel, and since then, I divide my time between the West

Coast, the East Coast, and the Middle East. I not only found inner peace, but dare I say—enlightenment. Today, I'm a better husband, better dad, and a better professional. I just feel like a better human all around, and I experience daily life in a very different way.

This book accompanies my coast-to-coast journey, providing a glimpse into the meditative experience of riding daily for hours. It also summarizes the insights that emerged from this experience along with the professional views of the experts. But more than anything, it is a book about dreams. Sometimes, a small shift in perspective demolishes the barriers, turns life around, and makes dreams come true. Today, my mission as a scientist, coach, and author is to help people make that shift and accomplish their most meaningful hopes and aspirations. This is what the book is really about.

I hope that this guide takes you on the ride of your life. Ride safe and ride on!

Ran Zilca
New York City, November 2013

HOW TO READ THIS BOOK

THE BOOK IS ORGANIZED IN CHRONOLOGICAL ORDER, ACCOMPANYING each day of the ride. As the solitary daily experience of riding continues, a shift gradually takes place in perspectives, thoughts, and mindsets. A shift that is reinforced by the personal stories of people I meet on the road, and a glimpse into the decisions they have made and into their life goals and aspirations. With each day, a new vantage point slowly emerges, and with it, new insights about life, its meaning, and the place inside where inner peace and inner strength reside. As we ride together, you may start vetting and reflecting on your life and how these insights apply to it.

The days when I met with experts are outside the normal rhythm of the ride. In fact, the expert interviews provide an opportunity to pause the experience and present a fresh set of thoughts to people who can enhance them with a body of relevant research, having studied similar concepts for a good number of years. The expert meetings, therefore, provide an analytic counterpart to the main volume of the book, which is more experiential in nature. If you'd like to keep the ride going and flow along with the experience, feel free to skip the interviews and go back to revisit them later.

The ride is divided into four parts:

Part I, Getting Lost: The first thirteen days of the ride, ending in Austin TX. This part is characterized by the chaos and confusion of leaving home and dealing with logistics, along with an attempt to define the experience and to understand it.

Part II, Getting Found: The third week of the ride, going from the vast planes of Texas all the way to Death Valley and California. This week was when everything sunk in. The effort to do things in one way or another was gone and gave way to a shift in perspective that will remain in effect until the end of the ride (and in the years to follow).

Part III, Getting There: The two days of riding through Yosemite and then arriving in San Francisco. This short part of the book is where a new person emerges after cocooning through the desert, and the pride over accomplishing the coast-to-coast goal is celebrated.

Part IV, Being There: Riding down the California coastline from San Francisco to San Diego, and conducting the final expert interviews, where the deepest concluding questions were asked.

PART I:
GETTING LOST

Day 0, September 18th:
New York — The Moment of Truth

THAT'S IT — THE MOMENT OF TRUTH IS HERE. IT'S 10:30 P.M. AND tomorrow the *Ride* begins. The motorcycle is all packed, and my laptop is buried in one of the bags in the back. I'm writing this on my phone. The luggage is pretty excessive and I'm worried about the extra weight in the back. I guess I will have to ride carefully for the first few days. An hour ago my wife walked into the garage as I was struggling with bungee cords, trying to hold all the bags together tightly. Her eyes gave a quick scan of the bike, then the bags, and finally me, standing barefoot in my boxer shorts, staring at her with a helpless expression. She lingered for another second and with no expression just said, "You can't go."

"I know," I said, "but I have to."

It was clear that by this time, the whole thing seemed like a bad idea. Earlier this afternoon, my four-year-old son, Ori, sat on the front steps of our house, gazing at the street and asking "to be by myself because I'm worried about daddy going away." That one I did not see coming. It broke my heart. By now, the kids are already sleeping, and my wife sits next to me on the living room couch. She sits quietly, pinned to the couch under the weight of her own silence. We both knew that I would be doing this, but now, in the drama of the night before, it feels like it came as a complete surprise. Perhaps the night before an adventure is always like this.

I must do this; there's no other way. Slowly, fear turns to excitement, and adrenaline is starting to rush through my bloodstream. My thoughts start to roam to the open road. I am actually going to be doing this.

Oh my God.

Day 1, September 19th: York, PA — Challenges and Strength

THINGS NEVER TURN OUT THE WAY YOU THINK. FOR MONTHS NOW, I've been picturing the first night on the road, but now, sitting at the motel room desk, I realize I was way off. Today's events, my whereabouts, and my emotional state are all completely different than I had previously imagined. I miss my wife and my kids and I toy with the idea of surprising them at home tomorrow, but a flood of excitement and pride masks my remorse. I am starting to realize the sheer scale of this journey.

The day started with saying good-bye. The kids gave me a big hug and went to Sunday school. It was especially nice to get a long hug from my eleven-year-old girl. She's already at an age when you can't squeeze a good hug out of her. I said goodbye to the neighbors, got on the motorcycle, and my wife followed me in the family van until we reached a gas station near the Tappan Zee Bridge. We spent another hour or so together, hugged, said our goodbyes, and then I left. The moment of departure was so shocking, so unreal, that it was impossible to cry. I've never been away from my family for more than a week, and the entire thing just felt like it wasn't happening.

During the first two hours, an unfamiliar feeling settles in my gut; a bland mix of panic, enthusiasm, regret, curiosity, and worry. It feels like I am the only one who's lost. Everyone else on the road knows where they're going. A guy on a yellow Honda Goldwing is going to meet his friends at a coffee shop. A family in a minivan is coming back home from a weekend getaway. A young couple in a red car is going to the city to hang out. I am the only one who doesn't know where he's headed. My throat shuts with anxiety, unable to contain the unexpected freedom. In the concrete lanes of I-78, I find myself becoming restless. I fidget in the seat and play with the music's volume, rushing the motorcycle in the left lane to catch up with the speeding train of my thoughts.

The road goes on, and the hours pass, and I start scanning the road for opportunities: Who will I meet today? Where will I eat? Will I join a group of bikers for a while? The possibilities seem endless. Anticipating my first adventure, I follow a sign at the side of the highway and take the next exit to a local restaurant. In the parking lot, there is a group of bikers, getting their bikes ready to go. This is it; I think. I'll park next to them. They will probably notice the large badge on the back of my jacket saying *"Ride of Your Life"* and engage me in conversation. Perhaps I'll join them for the next few hours. I park next to the group, but they pay no attention to me. They continue to speak among themselves and I can't think of anything to say. For a few moments, I stand next to the motorcycle and pretend to be checking it, hoping they'll approach me. They don't. Feeling childish and embarrassed, I get back on the bike and take off, heading again toward the highway.

Later on, I get off the interstate, and the world suddenly changes. On the side of Route 222, I see what I've been waiting for: endless corn fields and tall silos, the flatlands of Pennsylvania, a first glance into the real America. It is beautiful. My thoughts finally escape my mind. Everything vanishes apart from the soothing hum of the miles and the rolling pavement underneath the motorcycle's tires.

Only fifteen minutes go by before I decide to stop and take pictures. On the right, opposite a gas station, there's an office building on a hill. Its parking lot looks like it would have the perfect view, and I turn into the driveway and ride up to it. The view is indeed perfect. Excited, I swing my leg over to get off the motorcycle, only to realize that I forgot to push down the kickstand. It's too late. The motorcycle already leans left and its weight is pulling down. I hold on to the handlebars and try to pull it back up but to no avail. It continues to go down and falls gently on its side. I try to pick it back up, but it is too heavy. I stand and stare at it helplessly, lying on its side, with a little puddle of oil accumulating next to it, like it's been shot. I try to lift it again, panting and grunting, but it is no use. It is simply too heavy. In a futile attempt to get help, I go down the hill and stand on the side of the road, waving my arms up and down. None of the cars stop or even slow down. After twenty minutes of waving, I finally give up and cross the road to the gas station, not sure what to do. Next to one of the pumps, I spot a big guy with colorful tattoos on his arms. I ask him for help and luckily for me, he agrees. We cross the road together and pull the bike back onto its feet. I push the kickstand down and thank him. "It's my first day riding across the country," I say apologetically. He shrugs and says: "Looks like it's gonna be a rough ride." He is the first person I have spoken with since I left home. I check the motorcycle and am relieved to find that there's no damage except for a loose nut holding the right mirror. For the first time ever, I use the toolbox that is under the seat. I pull out a wrench and tighten the mirror.

I feel proud.

Just before sunset, I come across the Wright's Ferry Bridge, a ruler-straight beauty crossing the Susquehanna River. My first bridge. On the other side of the river, I find the Riverfront Bar & Lounge, a biker bar taken out of a movie scene. The windows are covered with dark curtains, and the air is filled with clouds of ciga-rette smoke that hover above poker and pool tables; the real deal. I ask for coffee to keep me awake. The bartender suggests Jell-O shots instead. I get a Diet Coke, drink it quickly, and leave. Perhaps, not the most exciting experience, but still, a biker bar on the first day. I am probably the nerdiest biker to have ever come here.

Later at night, I stop at the Best Western in York. Exhausted, fraz-zled, and sweaty, I carry the heavy bags on my shoulders to the room, passing by the hotel luggage cart several times without even noticing it. The buckles on the straps cannot hold the excess weight and they break. The bags fall off my shoulders. I have to make three trips to get them up to the room, carrying each bag in my arms like a baby. When I finish, I go back outside to clean the bike and check it. It's already dark outside. The receptionist is standing outside the front doors, smoking a cigarette, right next to the sign that says, "*thank you for not smoking.*" Her face has the indifferent, robotic expression that people sometimes have at work. Earlier, when I checked in, she was smiling, but the tone of her voice disclosed the emptiness that I now see in her. Is that what happens to you if you get stuck for too long? I walk to the Lyndon Diner across US-30. The food tastes great and the service is pleasant and easy going. I made it through the first day. Everything's fine.

Day 2, September 20th: Pennsylvania to Maryland — Attachment, Resilience, and the Power of Riding Aimlessly

THE FIRST DAY IS BEHIND ME — A MAJOR MILESTONE NOW CONQUERED. Filled with confidence and self-assurance, I leap out of bed, ready for adventure. Today, I think to myself, I will arrange everything upfront. No more surprises like yesterday. I start by following the routine I had originally planned: Thirty-minute walk, light breakfast, meditation, and then go to the motorcycle: check the air pressure, oil level, and brakes. Before taking off, I try to secure the bags again using bungee cords, but they simply won't hold. The luggage remains unbalanced and wobbly. A solution needs to be found. Yesterday, I felt the weight of the bags shift from side to side at each curve, and it's dangerous to continue this way. I ride to a local Auto Zone and ask for advice. They give me ratchet straps that can be fastened tightly each time I use them. I try them out and voila! The luggage stops moving around, solid as a rock. "Quality," I flatter myself, "just like in *Zen and the Art of Motorcycle Maintenance*." Satisfied that all is going as planned, I proceed to the first item on today's agenda: the Harley Davidson factory in York and from there on to the next item: Route 425. This back road is supposed to be my first local ride and was recommended by several motorcycling websites. My mood is high with anticipation as I navigate toward it, but strangely, as soon as I arrive, I am covered in a blanket of gloom. Something is wrong. But what is it? I continue to ride around and every now and then, stop to take pictures. The views are beautiful and the weather is inviting, but each time I maneuver the bike to stop and park I feel more and more depressed. I try to ignore it, but the feeling will not go away.

And then it occurs to me: too much planning. Instead of experiencing the road, I am trying to match it to my expectations and to document it with my camera; I am following a predetermined script made in the past and taking pictures for the sake of the future. The present moment completely disappeared. Realizing the mistake I made, I put the camera away and take a turn to a random side street, starting to ride aimlessly. Get lost. No destination and no plans. Suddenly, details surface from the scenery: fields, churches, schools, farms. An Amish buggy with three boys facing back at me, waving hello. The world is back. After a few hours of roaming, I stop at a gas station, find out where I am, and then head south toward Maryland. When traffic gets heavy, I take the next highway exit and let the road be my guide. Buddha said that the source of all human suffering is attachment, lack of flexibility, and the expectation that things remain the same. We desire permanence and become attached to our plans, not willing to accept that things always change. Starting tomorrow, I will embrace uncertainty. Allow the road to take me to new places. Come what may.

Day 3, September 21st: Bethesda, MD — Meeting with Coach Caroline Miller

CAROLINE MILLER AND I MET LAST YEAR AT THE FIRST WORLD Congress on Positive Psychology and since then, have been trying to find ways to work together. She is a successful life coach and one of the first graduates of the University of Pennsylvania's Master of Applied Positive Psychology program. Before she started helping others shift their lives, Caroline transformed her own: years ago she defeated an eating disorder and published a book about it, becoming an inspiration to thousands. Today, the focus of her work is the pursuit of personal goals and dreams. I could not have found a more suitable topic for my first interview.

I arrive at her house late in the morning, nervous, and tense. This is the first time I will be using the filming kit: two pocket video cameras on tripods, small lights on brackets, Lavalier microphones, and a pocket audio mixer. I hope it all works. I unpack, setup the gear, and run a few tests. Luckily for me, Caroline is a walking "positive intervention,"[1] and she makes me feel at ease, starting with her funky multi-colored nail-polish, through the bright yellow kitchen, to the needlework on the cushions saying "Carpe Diem." I decide to do just that — "seize the day," and as soon as the cameras roll, I forget about lighting and batteries and just allow the conversation to flow.

CONDUCTING A MIDLIFE REVIEW

My first question to Caroline is about midlife — a special period that is often dedicated to changes. The big question is how to harness this power of change to one's intentions rather than being drawn by change or resisting it.

This is such a great question. I do see this a lot in my work, and I cover some of this in *Creating Your Best Life*². There's a time in our lives when we biologically go through what's called a midlife review. This is when men and women start to take a look at their life and they assess their regrets. And regrets are very normal, and they're very common, and we all have them. However, in terms of well-being, one has two options: you either look at the regrets and you get more and more bitter, because you don't do anything to change it, you just live in the past and you ruminate: what if? What if I'd taken that job? What if I'd married that guy? On the contrary, other people who do a midlife review take those regrets and make changes in their lives — not just set goals but also create accountability to move toward those goals. Watching people give birth to midlife dreams is like watching babies being born. People regenerate themselves with big goals, and this is biologically the time people do it.

GOING ON THE ROAD

According to Caroline, people who find themselves in the midst of a midlife transition are often held back by different forces. People find it hard to chart a new path and are worried about failing or being misunderstood. Deep inside, they may actually know where they'd like to go, but the thought of leaving their comfort zone is too disturbing. Her advice is to adopt an optimistic mindset of success, "just get started," and take actions that lead to more action:

You may not realize how much power you actually have over your own destiny.

I think that in many ways, I was fortunate to hit my bottom in my early twenties with my eating disorder, because what brought me back to life was a twelve-step program that starts with the serenity prayer: "God, grant me the serenity to accept the things I cannot change; courage to change the things I can; and wisdom to know the difference." For many, many years, I listened to that prayer, and it really restructured my thinking in a really important time in my life when I was busy saving my own life. I did realize I had a lot of things I could control, including saving my own life that I hadn't thought I could.

The main reason I see holding people back is related to research by Locke and Latham on goal-setting theory and is simply that most people are afraid. They're not just afraid of change. They're afraid of everything: they're afraid of being looked at, not being looked at, being right, being wrong, being observed, being different. People end up being afraid of all kinds of things, and that's why most people stay stuck in "reactive ruts."

So, I think there's a lot of fear, but then there's the Petri dish that you live and work in, the people around you — do they have dreams? Do they change? Do they go after things that matter to them? Do they go outside of their comfort zone? The antidote to the fear is zest — a quality that is in abundance in children but declines rapidly by the time you're in your forties and fifties. You need a certain amount of zest, or joie de vivre. "Why not?" as opposed to "why?" A lot of people have that beaten out of them by life, by disappointments, by people who surround them.

"How do you activate or cultivate zest?"

The best approach is to keep an optimistic mindset while, at the same time, being mindful and aware of what is going on in front of you. When I was battling the eating disorder, I thought I was a victim of circumstance. That's the way pessimistic people think. They believe that when good things happen they got lucky and when bad things happen it was random. The world is a random set of events to pessimists. Optimists, on the other hand, believe they control the things around them. So, in some ways, you have to pretend you're an optimist. It's all about how you frame things. At the same time, you have to remain conscious and mindful of reality. Many of the people who survived the Sri Lanka tsunami were the fishermen who move slowly and cast their nets deliberately. They saw and felt the water rising before anyone else because they live so mindfully, and they went to higher ground. To be aware, we have to get quiet.

"How does being optimistic help you to get going? Do optimistic people enjoy the first steps they take?"

Armed with this mindful-optimistic mindset, you do have to just get started. And there's something about the risk/benefits ratio that I find interesting, which is: in the short term, we don't know exactly what's going to happen when we take risks. But when you take the first risks, you respect yourself more. There's some research called the "no pain no gain" research out of the University of San Francisco. What they've found is that when you go outside your comfort zone during the day, in an attempt to master something new or something you're trying to get better at, you'll actually be uncomfortable and unhappy while you're doing these things. But, at the end of the day, when you review your day, those are the things you're the proudest of. That is how you build self-esteem. That's how you build mastery, and ultimately, that's how you build lasting happiness.

Interestingly, this is exactly how I feel right now, on Day 3 of the *Ride*, sitting in Caroline's living room. These past three days have been tough on me, uncomfortable, and in many respects, unhappy, but the pride of being out there and doing it provides me with an unparalleled sense of satisfaction.

AVOIDING REGRETS

Toward the end of our conversation, Caroline tells me about an epiphany she had when her father passed away: at the end of life, people bitterly regret missed opportunities, but they rarely regret failed attempts. On a person's deathbed, the biggest possible regret is having missed out on the ride of their life:

That's what I ask when I talk to clients about risks they want to take: later in your life, will you regret not taking that risk? And instantly, if it's one of these core dreams, they say, "Yes — I have to do this." I must have heard this ten times today from clients who are talking about different dreams, and I said, "Well — are you ready to go for it?" "I have to do this to be authentic." You don't always see the rewards immediately but in the long term, people regret the risks they didn't take. In the short term, they regret the risks that didn't work out, but long term, looking back on their lives, when people do a life review, they regret the things they didn't have the nerve to go after.

And I really try to live my life like that. I have a personal story about this. My father died at 69, which is pretty young. And the one dream he articulated his whole life, which all three of his children knew about, was to retrace Odysseus' voyage. And he had books — a smart guy, Stanford graduate, he had the money, he had the time, he had the intellect, and he was passionate about it. And he died. And he died...because there was always another thing that he had to do at work — he was very successful at what he did. And when he died, all three of his children and his wife, the first thing that crossed all of our minds was, "Dad — why didn't you do it?" I was at the hospital just after my father died, and I was looking at him and the only thought I had was, 'you're never going to go around the Greek islands.' That was about ten years ago, and I think that it really caused me to focus my practice on "what is it you're meant to do here?" It doesn't have to be "curing cancer." It doesn't have to be earth-shattering to other people, but it has to be earth-shattering for your own life.

CAROLINE'S WISDOM:

- Pessimists believe that good things happen at random. Optimists believe they can affect things around them. Pretend to be an optimist
- When you go outside of your comfort zone, you may not initially feel great. During the day, you may be unhappy but at the end of the day you'll be the proudest
- At the end of a person's life, the regret of not-doing is far greater than regrets of failure
- Your dreams don't have to be earth-shattering to others, but they have to be earth-shattering to you

DAY 4, SEPTEMBER 22ND:
VIRGINIA TO NORTH CAROLINA —
BREAKING OUT AND LETTING GO

THE WEATHER FORECAST SAYS THAT IT IS GOING TO BE A VERY hot day. Definitely not suitable for a full-face helmet and a long-sleeved jacket. I pull the 'shorty' helmet and the leather vest out of the bags, put on sunscreen, and head down I-95, bare and exposed. Tonight's destination is Chapel Hill, NC, about three hundred miles south, so there will be plenty of riding in the sun. On the interstate, the lanes are filled with tractor-trailers surrounded by invisible bubbles of turbulent air. I ride between them cautiously, trying to avoid being pushed by the gusts. Through the speakers, a random shuffle is playing the best of the eighties: Judas Priest, Scorpions, Ozzy... The shorty helmet leaves my ears uncovered, and I can finally hear the music rise above the rumble of the engine, and with the jacket off, my bare arms can surrender to the heat of the sun. The road is unending and I lose all sense of time and space. Suddenly, I realize that I am singing along with the music at the top of my voice. My mind is empty. All thoughts have been flushed away and the ride is now synchronized to the sound coming out of the speakers. After turning onto I-85, the tractor-trailers are gone. The road is now decked with trees, bridges, and rivers. I turn off the music and allow time to come to a complete standstill. The world goes mute. Silent. I am motionless, but everything around me keeps moving.

At an unknown time in the afternoon, I wake up from the trance of the road, turn onto Interstate 40 and then Chapel Hill appears in the distance. More than four hours have gone by in an instant. I ride into town and think about the day's experience. It was a direct result of letting down my protective guards. The shorty helmet exposed me to a greater risk of injury in an accident, but it also allowed me to hear the music, feel the wind, and enjoy the road. The leather vest let in the sun and the wind, but it lacks the protection of the padded jacket. I wonder if this is something we do in life — wear shields of protection to keep us safe, at the expense of blocking our senses to life's full experiences. Over the years, a person moves to a house, buffered by land from the disturbance of neighbors. Defended from harm by airbags in the car and alarm systems at home, protected from embarrassment by social codes of conversation. The bigger the walls you build, the safer you are but also the more isolated, and when protection is excessive, the walls turn into a prison, The Bell Jar[3]. Once in a while, a person needs to break out, let go, and get a breath of fresh air. Air that is available only when you leave your safety zone and take some calculated risks.

In the evening, at the Chapel Hill Days Inn, there is a small pond with Koi fish. I walk next to it and notice that they follow my shadow. The fish expect to be fed when someone stands above them. They don't know what a person is, or that they are in a pond in a small hotel. All they know is that a shadow is usually followed by food. I stand and gaze at these beautiful fish. They swim within the borders of my shadow, careful not to leave it, waiting for a meal that doesn't come.

Day 5, September 23rd, Morning: Chapel Hill, NC — Meeting with Dr. Barbara Fredrickson

THIS MORNING, THE AIR IS HUMID AND UNPLEASANT, AND I AM ALL sweaty by the time I get to campus. Barbara is not there yet and I have time to set up the video equipment. Oddly, I still feel the heavy humidity inside the air-conditioned building; most likely a sign of my state of stress. I finish setting up early and sit down to wait. My leather vest, gloves, and bandana lay in a black pile on a chair, in stark contrast to the tidy, bright office.

"Open thinking" instead of "positive thinking"

When Barbara arrives, the first question I ask is about being present. She surprises me with a new way to look at the present moment.

It's true that bad is stronger than good — bad events affect us more than good events, but the other asymmetry that really goes under the radar most of the time is that good is much more frequent than bad. In the distribution of all the "nows," all of the present moments, by far most of these moments will be offering good experiences: the beauty of nature, the kindness of other people, interesting ideas to think about. I'd like to think of it as, "Well, if we really focus on the moment, like right this minute, is anybody putting pins in your eyes?" There's always something good in a situation.

Barbara is the director of the Positive Emotions and Psychophysiology (PEP) lab at the university's psychology department. We first met about a year ago and since then, had a chance to chat a few times about possible joint projects. Her first book, *Positivity*, describes various research studies on positive emotions that were conducted in her lab over the past few years. The findings are astounding in their simplicity and have to do with the number of positive emotions a person experiences during a day compared with the number of negative emotions, a ratio that is simply called "the positivity ratio." If that ratio equals three or higher, you eventually go into an "upward spiral" — a state of flourishing. If your daily dose of positive emotion is less than three times the negative, you risk going on a "downward spiral" into a negative state. Simply put, to flourish, you need to experience three times the good for anything bad.

Barbara's research also shows that "positive thinking" is not an effective strategy to become happier. Instead, it is more important to cultivate openness so that a person can recognize, notice, and appreciate the good that is already taking place in his or her life, and this way, tip the positivity ratio in his or her favor.

I think, actually, that when people learn about the science of positive emotions or the positivity ratio, there's a temptation to make your motto "I'm going to be positive." People think it will be easy. But I think that strategy backfires because there is a huge difference between genuine positive emotions and insincere positive emotions. Insincere positive emotions or even wishful-thinking positive emotions... sometimes we have insincere positive emotions because we want to make someone else think we're happy even though we really don't care: maybe it's the flight attendant saying goodbye to three hundred people leaving the plane, as part of a role. Other times, people learn about it and they so earnestly want to feel better that they strong-arm themselves into positive emotions, rather than changing their thinking or their behavior first. So, I think that a much better motto than "be positive" is "be open," or be appreciative and kind.

"Be open" does wonders because, especially in our contemporary culture, we are so caught up in mental time travel: ruminating about the past, or your mind telling you to think about this next thing that's coming in the future. We are constantly outside of the now. This is a great thing that humans can do, that other animals aren't able to — that mental time travel. It's a great human achievement, but it also robs us of the subtle experiences of goodness around us. I think that a really important strategy for being open is to just tune in to all of your senses: look at the trees, feel the breeze on your skin when you're on the motorcycle, just listening and really tuning in to what your senses are telling you. That's our quickest pathway into the present moment.

A STEADY DIET OF POSITIVE EMOTIONS

Barbara's work focuses on the dynamics of emotions over time, how emotions evolve and build, and how growing positive emotions can reach a point where they form a shield that blocks life's adversities. The dynamics go both ways: a "downward spiral" is characterized by a momentum of negative emotions — a contraction of openness to new experiences. On the other hand, an "upward spiral" is characterized by expansion of thought and an accumulation of positive emotions.

Negative emotions affect us more potently than positive emotions. Positive emotions are far milder, far subtler, far more diffused, and so, to stack up to the muscle power of negative emotions, they're going to need safety in numbers. There's not going to be a one to one — I can't undo or quell a negative emotion with just one positive emotion. Those positive emotions are in the moment, much subtler. Over time, they are extraordinarily powerful and they can change our character and build our resources, but the strength of positive emotions doesn't really emerge until you widen the time scope.

Emotions are processes that unfold over time, or experiences that unfold over time, and in a way, each emotion has a little bit of energy to reproduce itself in the next moment. If we are feeling sad or depressed, or hopeless, we encounter the next situation and we interpret it as a situation that has no hope. And that can bring us further and further down. There's interaction between the way emotions feel and how they affect our thinking that sends us either in a downward spiral (and that's been researched for decades), or more recently, we're finding that positive emotions and the expansive thinking that they lead to can create an upward spiral that perpetuates itself over time, where the good feelings spark open and flexible thinking allows you to see the good in more aspects of a situation. So the next moment is more likely to be positive than negative. Not to the point where you'd be oblivious to physical danger or anything like that — we don't have to worry about negative emotions becoming somehow unable to knock on our consciousness when we need them. But each emotion perpetuates itself in a self-sustaining system.

"How do these small bits of positive emotion add up? Can they really be the basis for personal transformation?"

Yes. That momentum is built because the slow and steady increments of positive emotions are fundamentally changing who we are. They're increasing the depth of our social network; they increase our resilience; they increase our ability to master our environment, and just handle day-to-day threats. A person who has experienced a wide range of positive emotions above the threshold of thriving, as a steady diet, has more tools on his or her tool belt to deal with difficult situations. It's a lot like physical health. A daily diet of fruits and vegetables contributes to how healthy you are going to be in the long run. I tell my kids this all the time: "Eating one piece of broccoli in October isn't going to be enough." You need to have a steady range of vegetables in your life, not just an occasional one. Positive emotions are the same way. We can't think "I'll have a weekend vacation next month and I'll just work like a dog until then." You need a steady diet of positive experiences and positive emotions. We can't put them off and recover once or twice a year on vacation.

MAKE YOUR OWN MOVIE

Even though this is only my fifth day on the road, some insights are starting to surface. One of them is the importance of "just doing it" — being proactive instead of observing things and analyzing them passively; Even if you're not exactly sure what to do, taking some sort of action is the best way to find out which way to go. Barbara agrees and hones in on the specific aspects of this notion:

I think that what makes a difference between, say, seeing a movie and doing a kind thing for another person is your own agency: you can take credit for it, and you can feel not only that you brought joy, or convenience, or some kind of relief to somebody else, but you can appropriately take credit for those actions. So there's a mixture of a number of emotions, including pride. Pride tends to get a bad reputation, but I think that when we do things that are virtuous, we should feel good about it because that reinforces future virtuous behavior. When agency is involved — when you control and make decisions about your good actions — there's a longer positive emotional yield because it's more complex. Don't watch the movie, make the movie!

MEDITATION AS A MEANS OF OPENING UP

Barbara's interest in meditation is both personal and professional. In her lab, she has conducted many studies on the psychological benefits of meditative practices, and in her personal life, she practices meditation on a regular basis. I ask her why she thinks meditation helps adopt a more open outlook (and, in turn, a higher positivity ratio).

When I first started bringing meditation into my research program, I learned a particular form of ancient meditation that's really about how to self-generate positive emotions. It's called "loving kindness meditation." The kind of meditation that's been studied the most in the West in recent years is related to sitting and focusing on one's breath. In loving kindness meditation, you also start by focusing on your breath — but especially the heart region. It's also a concentration practice, but instead of concentrating on your breath, you focus on a handful of classic phrases that are intended to help evoke warm and tender feelings toward others. Starting with people you already feel warm and tender feelings for or a pet, somebody who, when you think of them, it just makes you smile. You think of that person and the classic phrases of love and kindness are "may you be safe," "may you be happy," "may you be healthy," "may you live with ease." Those are the touchstones, but the aim is to set your intention to actually feel those emotions. And just get practice in self-generating those feelings. Have them just be like the weather: "Oh, I can feel warm and tender feelings when that person comes into my view, but I'm not able to feel that unless they're here." So it's kind of learning that we have more control over our emotions than we think and that we can turn them on and turn them off and also cultivate them with our actions.

In saying these phrases, you're not trying to do some "magical thinking" and make their lives perfect. It's really about conditioning your own heart so that when you encounter other people, eventually it extends the practice to include people you don't feel anything about normally, people you don't even know, and the idea is changing the habitual way of thinking about people so that when you encounter a new person whom you haven't met before it's more likely that you will be wishing him or her well and caring about the person than thinking "well…"

YOU ALREADY HAVE INNER PEACE

When our meeting comes to a close, I ask Barbara about inner peace — the purpose of my own journey.

I think that there are tremendous slings and arrows and threats that come to us in daily life that get us to be very self-protective, that get us to be very self-focused, and make us concerned about ourselves. So you don't even notice the cashier in the supermarket, you literally see her as an obstacle to getting out the door, instead of a person who is feeling her own complicated set of emotions at the time, and yet, when we realize that in this present moment "no one is putting pins in your eyes" — why should we be self-protective in a safe situation? For many of us, many more moments are safe than we acknowledge and that allows this other focus to blossom, this chance to experience and express love, to really see the other person, and build from that.

BARBARA'S WISDOM:

- Bad affects us more than good, but good is far more frequent than bad
- Being present means being open to receiving this good that exists most of the time
- Over time, a "steady diet" of positive emotions transforms a person and builds resilience
- Be proactive about life. Don't watch a movie — make one!
- Adopt a practice like loving kindness meditation, helping you condition your heart, and see that we're all the same
- Inner peace is within reach when you simply remind yourself that you are safe

DAY 5, AFTERNOON: WAR PIGS, SUPERMAN, AND MY NEW FRIEND STEVE

RIDING THROUGH THE SCENIC BACK ROADS FROM CHAPEL HILL TO Greensboro feels like a trip back in time. The road twists between pickup trucks, horses, and cowsheds. Ozzy is cranking on the speakers with "War Pigs," and all of a sudden, I am filled with a sense of great pride. The luggage is tied up tight in the back with the new ratchet straps, the video gear worked fine and I've already shot two interviews, I know my way through the back roads, and have greater confidence in my riding. I am really doing this.

After leaving Burlington and heading north on Route 220, the villages become smaller and the curves of the road become more twisty. At some point, it feels like the bike disappears from underneath me and I am hovering over the curves with hands stretched forward on invisible handlebars, just like Superman, alternating between left and right twists in a slow, constant rhythm. Right before reaching Roanoke, the breeze becomes chilly and smells sweet, and I sense the presence of the mountains ahead. And then, minutes later, they erupt in front of me in all of their majestic might. Layers of massive earth formations hiding behind each other, standing like royal guards protecting the setting sun. It feels like all cars on the road are going together toward them. Riding together in a single file, like a group of pilgrims.

By the time I get to Roanoke, it's almost dark. I arrive at the motel at the same time as three other bikers from Kentucky, and we strike up a conversation about the Blue Ridge Parkway. When they check in, I observe the reception guy speaking with them. He goes out of his way to help the guys, talking with them about their trip, trying to understand if there is anything extra they need. Then, when my turn comes to check in, he gives me directions and recommendations, and asks where I came from and where I am headed. For this receptionist, work is not a job, it is a calling, an opportunity to help the travelers who stop at his doorstep.

After unpacking, I go to the front desk and ask him if they have any coffee. At first, he suggests that I use the coffee maker in my room. Then, pauses for a second, looks at me, and says, "Ahhmmm... screw it – I just brewed a fresh pot, hold on." He goes into the kitchen and comes back with a fresh cup, and we start talking. A self-described "super nerd" and "news junky," Steve is only 22 but has the knowledge and personality of a university professor. We talk about TV, the media, and politics, and then go out for a cigarette. After lighting up, the conversation turns more personal and he tells me about his demons and his dreams. He is an alcoholic and has been sober for two years. He attributes his addiction to a fear of adulthood — a fear of being stuck in a meaningless career and meaningless grown-up life, like his father was. As a child, Steve watched his dad forgo his dreams for a job he disliked and for a life to which he was indifferent. Steve vows to live differently and spend his life in pursuit of his dreams. Appropriately for a super nerd, he is working on a new kind of *Dungeons and Dragons* game, a version that would be ten times more complicated than any of the games that are out on the market today. He describes his game idea to me in detail, then pauses, and for the first time since we met, the smile leaves his face: "the thing is," he says "I don't know if game companies would be interested in a game that is so complicated. Perhaps, I should dumb it down a little. You know, just to make it a little friendlier." He waits for my response. I am living my dream and riding across the country, so in this conversation, I am the dream expert. I hesitate for a second. "Tell you what," I finally respond, "I find it hard to believe that you are the only super nerd in this world. If you find this new game exciting, then it must be that every single super nerd out there will be excited about it too. So, I think you should make it crazy-sick complicated, and when you pitch it to game companies, say explicitly that you are focusing on this new super-nerd audience. What do you think?" A cloud is lifted from his face. "Yes," he says, "I will do just that!" and the conversation continues until one of the guests appears at the door, and Steve joyfully goes back to serving his guests.

DAY 6, SEPTEMBER 24TH: BLUE RIDGE PARKWAY — THE MOUNTAINS, THE PASTOR, AND WORLD PEACE

THE TV IN THE MOTEL BREAKFAST-ROOM IS SHOWING IRANIAN President Ahmadinejad speaking to the United Nations' General Assembly. He claims that the 9/11 attacks were a US conspiracy and calls it "an inside job." I remember the morning of September 11th 2001. When the first plane crashed into the World Trade Center, I was driving my daughter to preschool in the New York suburbs. She was two years old and still our only child. My wife and I were newcomers to the country and had moved only a few months before. I remember the shock, the horror, and the chaos of the days that followed. The military Hummers and helicopters in the city, the concern for friends who work downtown, the uncertainty, and the disbelief. Ahmadinejad's speech continues to play in the background and most people do not pay attention to it. I chat with the bikers from Kentucky and at the same time, think about the Iranian president. In a few weeks, I will be meeting with Phil Zimbardo, who ran the Stanford Prison Experiment back in 1971. In the forty years that passed since then, the foci of Zimbardo's research have been the understanding of evil behavior. If he's watching the news right now, I wonder what he's thinking. Is Ahmadinejad really evil?

When I get on the Blue Ridge Parkway, the morning chill is still in the air, and the road is different than I had imagined it: narrow and twisty, and hard to maneuver with the bags in the back. I wrestle with the motorcycle in the turns, trying to manage its lean-angle and keeping the weight balanced. After thirty minutes of body language, I finally adjust to the road and my mind becomes available to absorb its beauty. The vegetation and topography keep changing and surprise me with new colors, textures, and scents. I feel like I am riding a Star Wars speeder bike[4] in between the trees of a distant planet.

The surrounding mountains in the background are primal, the landscape of creation. At some point, I see colorful flakes in the air. At first, they look like autumn leaves, but then I realize that they are butterflies. The air is filled with them. A snowfall of swallowtail butterflies.

After a few hours, I pull over to one of the overlooks at the side of the road and stop next to a car. Its engine is shut off and a man is sitting in the driver's seat, having his breakfast. He and I are the only ones here, and I ask him if he minds taking my picture. We chat a little, and it turns out that he is a pastor at a local church, and that he often comes to this overlook to meditate and pray. He says that he was born in the mountains and wants his ashes to be spread in the mountains when he dies. We talk about the spiritual ambience of this place; how the presence of something greater, divine, is felt in every piece of the scenery here. Strangely, when we part ways, it feels like we've known each other for years and will see each other again soon. I continue to ride down the parkway and my mind is filled with the imagery around me, blended with thoughts about good and evil, and about the presence of God. Conflicts dwarf in the shadow of these mountains. This here is a place of peace.

A place of solutions. Out of nowhere, a picture appears in my mind. I imagine Ahmadinejad and president Obama riding the Parkway together. Ahmadinejad rides a Trike (a cool custom kit) and Obama is on a touring machine — something like a Road Glide[5]. Both men wear black shorty helmets, sunglasses, and tough facial expressions. A Def Leppard[6] song is pumping in full volume from one of their motorcycles. After riding for a few hours straight they pull over at Bluffs Restaurant and get off their bikes, exhausted, but all wired up. They share a drink of water from a plastic bottle and Ahmadinejad says, "You know, I don't even remember what I was upset about." Obama responds, "I have no idea either," and then they go inside the restaurant and devour cheeseburgers with salty fries. If we want world peace, possibly all we have to do is get our leaders together on a few weekend rides right here. In a couple of weeks, the notion of war will become obsolete.

At night, I arrive in Linville, North Carolina, and park the bike at the Pixie Inn, an old-fashioned motel close to Grandfather Mountain. The owner is a woman in her late seventies and has been running the inn for more than fifty years. Her office has no computer — all registration is done using paper forms. On the wall behind the front desk, there's a picture of President Ronald Reagan (and she says: "they don't make men like that anymore"). I get to choose between an "old room" (built in the 1950s) and a "new room" (built in the 1980s), which is $5 extra. Linville is a small town — a couple of restaurants and one gas station. There is no cell reception, no Wi-Fi, and no broadband signal. On the desk in the room, there's a rotary phone. The place is clean and well run. When I ask the owner about laundry, she takes me to the staff laundry room where they wash the towels and sheets. She is open, grounded, warm, firm, alert, and industrious. She is also happy and full of love. Not in an obvious, cheerful kind of way, just content with her life and looking for ways to help her guests. She doesn't smile, but her face shows no sign of remorse or regret. She's immersed in the moment, amazingly strong, responsible, and does not judge anyone. Simply put, she is the mother of all guests in this motel. I follow her to the laundry room and make a mental note to myself, "You can run the same business in the same tiny town for fifty years and still be on the ride of your life."

Day 7, September 25th:
From the Pixie Inn to Dollywood

THE ONLY PLACE AROUND HERE THAT OFFERS INTERNET ACCESS IS a small coffee shop in Newland called The Ugly Mugg. It's Saturday morning and the place is buzzing with people: families with children on their way to soccer games, young couples, an old man with an old pickup truck, and the local dentist who knows everyone in town. I get a fresh cup of coffee and set my laptop on one of the tables, get wired in, and start backing up and uploading yesterday's video files and notes. After an hour of work, I reluctantly leave to go out and answer the call of the road. As I stow the computer in the back of the motorcycle, I notice that the sky is getting darker with clouds. The old man in the pickup truck says he's pretty certain that it will pour today. He says he feels it in "them bones." I head north on Route 194. My mind is preoccupied with the chances of rain, but the scenery pacifies me, and before long, I stop thinking about it and surrender myself to the road.

An hour later, on I-81, a few dots of rain start to collect on the windshield. After a week on the road, the long-dreaded rain has finally come. This is the moment I've prepared for, I tell myself. I've never ridden in the rain before, but I'm ready. I pull over on the side of the road and start suiting up. I release the straps on the bags in the back, take the gear out, put on the rain suit, and sit on the pavement to put on the rain boots. Then, I buff the helmet visor with rain repellent, and finally, I'm ready to go. When I get back on the highway, I feel awfully prepared; only that in the meantime, the rain had stopped. The windshield is dry, and the clouds have all dissipated. A few miles down the road, I stop at a gas station to fuel up. It is stiflingly hot in the rain suit and the boots make a funny squeak when I walk. Just then, a loud Harley pulls in next to me. The rider is wearing a thin t-shirt with an imprint of the Marine Corps on it, and his head is covered with a small skull-cap[7]. We chat and he tells me that he's on his way back from a camping trip in California. He has no bags on his bike. Everything is stored in his motorcycle's tiny trunk. I look at the mess of bags on my motorcycle and feel the sweat inside my rain suit start to steam up from my collar. The contrast between the two of us is stark: I'm the dork with the midlife crisis wearing a pair of rain boots in perfectly dry weather. I stay at motels, navigate using my mobile phone, and carry a laptop. He defies the rain and camps out every night. I'm pretending to be him for a few weeks. He's simply him.

A couple of hours later on I-40 outside of Knoxville, I decide to end the day early. My cue is a sign next to exit 407 that says "Dollywood." I take the exit to Smoky Mountain and head off to find a place to spend the night.

Day 8, September 26th: Tennessee, Georgia, Alabama — What Doesn't Kill You Makes You Wet

THE CLARION INN IN SEVIERVILLE IS BUILT LIKE A PLANTATION house, as a tribute to the movie *Gone with the Wind*. The walls are decked with pictures of Clark Gable and Vivien Leigh, and as I walk through the hotel, I keep thinking about the famous film line: "Frankly, my dear, I don't give a damn." What a line. It's a shame that there's never a good opportunity to say it out loud in real life. This land is Dolly Parton's land. Just like the exit sign on the highway promised yesterday, Dollywood is only a few miles away, and Dolly's face is on brochures at the reception desk, on billboards at the side of the road, and on the back of my room key. This mix of Dolly with *Gone with the Wind* makes the place really fun.

Today, the rain finally arrived with all of its might. I sit in the room and stare at it falling on the balcony window, trying to figure out whether to go out and to continue riding south. Do I trust myself to keep safe and avoid getting injured? What if I discover that I cannot handle the rain? What if the bag covers let water in and damage the computer and video equipment? I check the weather forecast again. It shows constant rain for the next three days. It doesn't look like I have a choice. The only way to escape this rain is to ride away from it. I go out and start preparing: put the rain covers on the bags; strap the bags tightly with the ratchet straps; and wear the rain jacket, pants, and boots. Unlike yesterday, today is not a drill, and it feels comforting to be suited-up and protected. As I prepare the motorcycle for the road, hotel guests pass by and some of them stop to talk and share a story. They are curious about the lone biker from New York and are in no rush to leave in the rain. I stall for another hour and talk with some of them. When they leave and say goodbye, they wish me well and ask me to keep safe. Their faces are serious, and their request is an honest plea of concern, not a courtesy. I am starting to get more and more nervous.

The rain gets stronger and I have to get moving. I mount the bike and head out on the gravel road leading out of the hotel, grateful to be reaching solid pavement at the end of it. A million tiny raindrops fire needles into my thighs, piercing through the rain suit and the jeans. The downpour is so heavy that it feels like I am submerged, riding through solid screens of water. Everything feels different. The grip of the tires is weaker, the visibility is poor, and the weight in the back pushes things out of balance constantly. Surprisingly though, water does not penetrate the clothes and I am dry inside. I focus all senses on the road, realizing that I can't afford to miss a single pebble, puddle, or passing car. The effort takes up all of my attention, leaving no room for fear or worry, and by the time I reach the interstate, I am starting to adjust to the demands of the slippery road. The miles pass by and I gradually feel more confident. I slowly speed up to a safe sixty miles per hour and continue to ride steadily, constantly monitoring the state of the road, the state of traffic, and my state of mind. The road goes on, drowning in wet, grey rain. I'm holding up, but the level of challenge is clearly above my level of riding skill.

A few hours later, the rain remits for a short while, and my head frees up to think. The thought of riding in the rain was distressing, but that is exactly why I feel so proud right now. This is what Barbara Fredrickson talked about when we met earlier this week: challenge and risk are cornerstones of happiness. In our society, we spent the previous Century in an attempt to relieve people of the challenges of life. Comfort has become a value, a dream, something to strive for. But we have mistaken comfort for happiness. Challenges, in fact, are the fuel for the ride of your life. They bring self-esteem, satisfaction, autonomy, and pride. To live means to sweat, push, fail, and then push even harder. To live means to empty the dishwasher with your kid, assemble a piece of furniture you bought, or plow through a difficult meeting at a job that you love. The confrontation of challenge and the embracing of risk are the essence of life itself. Comfort kills.

I pass Georgia into Alabama on I-59 where a large sign tells me that I've now entered the Central Time Zone. Today, I rode through three states and two time zones, in a bath of rain. I feel great.

DAY 9, SEPTEMBER 27TH: ALABAMA TO MISSISSIPPI — A BITTERSWEET BIRTHDAY, AND A MEETING WITH OMAR

WHEN I WAS PLANNING THE *RIDE* AND DECIDING WHEN TO LEAVE, I had to take the weather into consideration. If I left too early, I would have to ride in temperatures reaching 110 degrees when I reach Death Valley. Leaving too late, I could hit snow or icy pavement in the mountains. For a five-week trip, this left very little choice of schedule. I decided to leave a week after Labor Day and come back at the end of October. The only drawback of this plan was that I would have to be away on my son's eighth birthday, which is today.

The plan was to postpone his birthday party until my return and give him an early birthday present before I depart. A few weeks ago, he and I spent a day in the city together and went to FAO Schwartz[8] to choose his present. After searching in the different departments, we decided to go for a custom Muppet. Tomer chose a goatee and a black biker jacket for his Muppet and named him Lucas. It was a perfect gift and a perfect day. I thought that I was okay with this. But this morning, waking up a thousand miles away, in Rainbow City, Alabama, it feels awful not to be home. I can't help thinking that Lucas is a plush version of myself, a toy that was meant to replace my son's lost father, who has abandoned him.

The first thing I do when I wake up is call home to wish Tomer a happy birthday. His voice sounds happy and thrilled. A few days ago, a local newspaper ran an article about me, and he saw it last night. Now, he cannot contain his excitement. "You are in the paper daddy! And they have a picture of you on your motorcycle!" Tomer goes on to tell me about the cupcakes he is bringing to school today, and I tell him how yesterday I rode in the rain. The call goes well. He is in a good mood and sounds excited and happy. But when I hang up the phone, I still feel like I bribed him into losing something that is rightfully his. The guilt won't go away.

I get a quick breakfast at the motel and start preparing for today's ride. The pace of the past few days has been slower than expected, and I need to stay on the interstates to catch up. The plan is to continue on I-59, loop onto I-459 around Birmingham, and get as close as possible to New Orleans. I leave the bags in the lobby and ride to a gas station next door to fuel up. I stop by the pump and when I take off, the helmet falls on the ground. It makes a sudden, loud cracking sound, and the internal sun visor breaks. I pull the visor out, take a long useless look at it, and throw it in the garbage. Motorcycle helmets are "one time" — the impact could break the internal protective materials, so a helmet needs to be replaced once it is dropped. It's a disturbing thought, but I dismiss it immediately and irresponsibly. I put the helmet back on, ride back to the hotel, and start loading the bags onto the motorcycle. When I tie one of the straps, I pull it too hard and the buckle breaks. This is not good. My gear has to last me another month on the road. I can't afford to drop helmets and break buckles.

I must pull myself together and to cut myself some slack. I step aside, pull out a cigarette, close my eyes, and take a few minutes to call together a collage of my best moments with my son. I think of the time we assembled the computer desk together, how we play ball in the yard, or have breakfast at the Pleasantville Diner. I remember how he sounded excited and proud when we spoke earlier. Slowly, my confidence comes back. Lucas the Muppet is not a substitute for a lost father. He is, in fact, a tribute to a role model. I am a hero to my son. He's okay. We're okay It's all good.

I go back to the motorcycle, tie a knot around the broken buckle, and take off.

A couple of hours into the day, the rain weakens. The road is open, and I give in to it and let it carry me south. The relief from the rain fills my body with joy. A sweet smell of damp leaves is in the air, and dark clouds in the sky are slowly sailing east, leaving behind them a clean world of shiny shrubs and clean pavement. Time stands still again and I forget what day it is, what time it is, and where I am.

By the afternoon, all that is left of yesterday's storm is a drizzle, and the pavement is almost dry. Near Tuscaloosa, I stop at a gas station to fuel up and stretch. It's a huge station but completely deserted. Inside, an attendant sits behind a counter. He is a young man, dark, slender, and short, with blazing brown eyes. When he hears that I rode all the way from New York, he stands up and asks to take a look at the motorcycle. We go outside and I take a picture of him sitting on it. We stand and chat, enjoying the unexpected break from the solitary quiet of the rainy day. There are no customers and there is no rush, and after speaking for some time, we go back inside and have lunch together. This stranger I just met, working two gas-station jobs in southern Alabama, is a man in pursuit of his dreams. His name is Omar. When he was three years old, his family moved to the US from Saudi Arabia and settled in an Arab-American neighborhood close by. Even though he grew up in the country, Omar says that he always felt like an outsider, and he hopes that his young son's experience will be different from his own. His dream is to write a book that will help young American Arabs bring together their ethnic and national identities and open a door for them into American society. His current job, working shifts in gas stations, earns him enough to save for college, so that sometime in the future, he can get the education he needs to start writing his book. Sitting behind the counter today, Omar is, in fact, in the midst of chasing his dream. One can see it in his eyes and hear it in his voice. He is on fire.

Note: a year after I met Omar, severe tornados hit Tuscaloosa, flattening entire neighborhoods, and taking several lives. I pray and hope that Omar and his close ones are all well and safe and that he is continuing his journey.

Late in the afternoon, I park the bike at the Super 8 motel in Laurel, Mississippi. My wife and I decided to have a video call with the kids tonight, to celebrate Tomer's birthday, and time is tight. I unpack, go back on the bike, and head out to get a quick dinner at a Pizza Buffet down the road. I promise myself to go easy on the food, but I end up eating mountains of it. Outside, in the parking lot, as I stand next to the motorcycle and put on the gloves, I hear a female voice say: "nice bike." I look around but can't see where it is coming from. I slide the key into the switch and then hear it again: "I like the way it looks." It is the voice of an old lady, coming from a few feet away, but I can't see her. I look around again, more closely this time, and notice a woman sitting in a car, smiling, about twenty feet in front of me. I smile back at her, and she continues to share her story: "My husband and I used to ride for many years. We used to go out on weekends. He had a Goldwing trike[9]. Yellow. I can't recognize what type your bike is. Is it a metric?"[10] I tell her it's a V-Star 950, much smaller than a Goldwing. "I remember the experience," she says, "the wind going through your hair, being out in the open. We both really used to love it. He is ill now, so we stopped riding a few years back, but it was really fun." I listen to her and say, "Once a rider, always a rider." She nods in agreement.

"Did you ride all the way from New York?"

Yes, it was always a dream of mine. Life is short. Decided to do it.

"I have a sister in New York. Upstate. I haven't spoken with her in a while though. It's a long story. I guess you're right. Life is short. Maybe I'll give her a call. Have a good one. And you be careful now. okay?"

It's time to head back. I stop by a grocery store next to the motel, and get half a caramel cake, disposable spoons, and a plate. In the motel room, I place the cake on the table and make a video call home. Tomer cuts a slice from his birthday cake at home, and I cut a slice of mine, and we all eat together. He laughs really hard when he hears that I bought the cake at the "Piggly Wiggly."[11] He thinks I made the name up. After the party, I go out and start cleaning the motorcycle. It's all dirty after riding in the rain the past two days. I rub the wheel spokes, wax the fuel tank, and work lotion into the seats. At the end, I take a picture of it, capturing the shine of the chrome. I go to bed full of pride. It was a good day.

Day 10, September 28th: New Orleans — Frog Legs and Weeping Guitars

EACH NIGHT SO FAR, I SLEPT LIKE A BABY AND WOKE UP BRIGHT and early. But tonight, the energy rush of the past ten days is finally down, making way for an adrenaline crash. I am exhausted. Sitting in a hotel room a block away from the legendary Bourbon Street in New Orleans, I am trying to gather some energy to write. For the first time since I left home, I realize that I desperately need to rest.

Leaving Laurel this morning towards Biloxi, the weather was sunny and bright and the mood was high: The rain is finally gone; the sky is deep blue, and the bike is shiny and clean. On the handlebar speakers, distorted guitars are shredding along, and the late Ronnie James Dio screams his lungs off, asking someone to "*lock up the wolves.*" I find myself dancing again in the seat, standing on the floorboards, and getting high on a fresh supply of wind. When I reach Biloxi, I stop for lunch and take a few pictures. The ocean in front of me is aquarelle blue, and the smell of fried seafood is carried on the wings of a warm breeze. Five years have passed since Hurricane Katrina, but the trauma is far from forgotten, and the subtle remains of it are everywhere. The waitress at the restaurant tells me about the storm and its aftermath. She was thirteen when it hit, and she remembers it through the eyes of a child. In bleak contrast to the scenic view of the ocean behind her, her stories describe homelessness, crime, and poverty. Her sadness is contagious, and my heart sinks. I rush to pay and leave.

It's time to head west toward Louisiana. Back on Interstate 10, swarms of guys on Harleys are on the road, riding west. I sail the right lane at seventy five miles per hour and they all pass me. Most of them don't bother to do "the wave."[12] They push the engines to their limits and forge forward, leaning right and left to switch lanes. As the miles go by, I start to feel the excitement building up in my abdomen, then rise slowly to my throat. Tonight, I will reach New Orleans, the most southern point of the Ride, and start heading straight west, through the Gulf and the Bayou, into the depth of Texas. With ten states and a few thousand miles behind me, I am well beyond the point of no return. I have already mastered the gear, the logistics, the first interviews, and the heavy rain. This *Ride* is starting to become a part of me. The never-ending road, the roar of the motorcycle, the wind, the sun, and the rain, all penetrated my skin, leaving less room for the mind to plan, simulate, or analyze. The voice in my head is quiet. I feel stronger, more deferential, and present.

An hour later, I find myself riding along Lake Pontchartrain into New Orleans. There's something remarkable about encountering something this grand without expecting it. The thin bridge lies very low, surrounded by water all the way to the horizon. The feeling is agoraphobic, floating with no anchor, sailing on the surface of the lake.

As soon as I get to New Orleans, I go to a bar at the corner of Conti and Bourbon, at the heart of the French Quarter. The sun is still out, and the place is almost empty. A band is standing in the corner, playing George Thorogood songs. I get a beer at a Happy Hour price, and sit down to listen. Song after song, the guitar riffs cut through the air in a sharp, weeping sound. The sun sets slowly in the open windows, and the beer continues to flow. I've always dreamt of playing the Blues on Bourbon Street. I wish I could stand in the corner and play with them. When they take a break, I gather my courage and approach them. I ask if I can join for one song. They refuse. Surprisingly, I feel relieved.

DAY 11, SEPTEMBER 29TH: CROSSING THE BAYOU FROM LOUISIANA TO TEXAS

NEW ORLEANS IS MAGICAL THIS MORNING, AND IT IS STILL ASLEEP. No one stands on the balconies of the famous Creole Townhouses,[13] and the streets are empty. The motorcycle crawls through the narrow alleys quietly and respectfully, slowly breaking out toward the highway. Within minutes, we are outside of town, riding on the edge of Lake Pontchartrain, in the hazy swamp that surrounds the city. An array of tall, naked trees stick out of the brown water around the road, a reminder that this is Bayou Country — strange, bewitched, and mystical.

A mere hour later, after crossing the mighty Mississippi, the road rises up and becomes detached from the ground. Supported by poles that are stuck in the swamp, it turns into the Atchafalaya Basin Bridge. It is over eighteen miles long and raised high above the bayou. A few minutes after entering it, everything disappears. All you can see around you is the pavement shooting into the horizon both in the front and back, and the steam coming up from the swamp deep underneath, where alligators lurk. The experience is both exhilarating and troubling. The two lanes are narrow with no shoulder, and a short concrete railing at the side of each of them guards the vehicles from falling into the abyss below. My attention is dedicated to keeping a safe distance from this railing, and to watching the side-winds and the passing trucks. I also need to battle my fear of heights and the confused perception of riding in the middle of the sky.

About halfway through the bridge, an exit sign points to the Atchafalaya Welcome Center. I lean on the handlebars to push the motorcycle onto the ramp, so I can take a break from the strenuous riding. Down below, there is a vast, empty parking lot.

I pull over, keep the engine running, and get off the bike. A random song is playing through the speakers. I take off my gloves and touch the screen on my phone, looking for Creedence Clearwater Revival's *Born on the Bayou*.[14] Within seconds John Fogerty's voice rips through the silence of the empty parking lot:

> *"I can remember the fourth of July, runnin' through*
> *the backwood bare.*
> *And I can still hear my old hound dog barkin'*
> *chasin' down a hoodoo there*
> *Born on the Bayou*
> *Born on the Bayou"*

A friendly biker wearing a blue bandana approaches me. He ignores the music and doesn't notice the intended relevance of the song's lyrics. We stand around and chat for some time, and he suggests that I check out the visitor center. I take his advice, turn the engine off, and head in. Inside, there is an audio-visual presentation about the area's wildlife, and a coffee machine. A guy is putting coffee beans in it. His sleeves are rolled up, exposing a set of tattoos on his forearms. A biker. He and I stand by the coffee machine and talk about our riding trips and about the custom kits he's put on his Fat Boy[15]. It feels great to be a part of this network of bikers spread across the country.

I get back on the bridge, this time more prepared for it, leaning into the ramp in anticipation. In the remaining miles I am able to take my mind off the risk, and simply enjoy the experience.

Past Lafayette, the interstate continues in a straight line, piercing through the green grass of Louisiana's West Gulf Coastal Plain. Two peaceful hours pass-by, and then a small sign announces the Texas state-line. As a child, I imagined Texas to be the home of cowboys; the place where heroes ride wild horses with revolvers hanging from their belts. Thirty years later I am here, riding my own horse of steel.

Day 12, September 30th:
Thoughts of a Temporary Nomad

THIS MORNING, I DECIDED TO TAKE A BREAK FROM THE INTERSTATE. I started the day on Farm to Market Rd 1131, a peaceful country road just north of Vidor. It was everything I've gotten to love about off-interstate America: Farms with tall silos, family-run gas stations, and old churches. From there, I went back on I-10, straight into the futuristic interchanges of Houston, which spit me out onto Route 71. In the afternoon, the endlessness of Texas finally appeared. For three hours, I rode silently alongside the Texas Colorado River, until I reached Austin at night.

More than ten days and twenty six hundred miles have passed since I went on the road. The days now have a familiar rhythm of routine, starting with loading and securing the gear and ending with finding a place, doing the laundry, video chatting with the family, and writing. Being out in the sun gave me a dark tan, with glove lines on my wrists and a goggle-shaped "tan mask" on my face. My clothes and boots are starting to wear out, and anyone who sees me knows that I am on a long journey. I am starting to feel like a nomad, a "big log."[16] With no meetings or calendar to follow, the clock has become meaningless, and the time of day is now determined by the position of the sun. All of my attention, focus, and energy are dedicated to figuring out how much gas I have left in the tank, finding the nearest spot to have a meal, and looking for a place to spend the night. During the day, with all channels of the mind occupied with these tasks, there is no room left to think of anything else, and, therefore, no room for worry.

Close to the midpoint of this *Ride*, right before hitting the long stretch through Texas, is a good time to contemplate the experience, and to check the pulse for changes. The first thing I notice is that my natural pace has gone down. I walk more slowly, speak more slowly, and probably think more slowly. I am also surprised to discover that I am much more quiet than usual. I interact with many people during the day (everyone talks to a biker with out-of-state plates), but when in conversation, I am more concise and stingy with my words. Proportions and perspectives have adjusted to fit the unending size of the country. The daily concerns that once occupied me have shrunk in comparison to the vastness of the *Ride* and the infinite length of the road. Troubles are small and the world is big and inviting.

Day 13, October 1st: Austin, TX — Hindu Wisdom, Powerful Words, and the BS of Psychology

Barsana Dham is a polished gem nestled in the back roads of Hill Country. It resides in a beautiful white building decorated by fine replicas of artwork from India and surrounded by ponds and gardens. Having never been to a Hindu temple before, I am not exactly sure what to expect, although I have some rough knowledge of Hinduism. A few years ago, I read a translation of the Upanishads (the ancient Hindu scriptures) and came away with three major principles:

(1) Live life in the present.
(2) Recognize that all is connected, and
(3) Focus on the action or "job," instead of outcome.

Similar notions are found in modern psychology, and I wonder if there will be similarities between what I hear at Barsana Dham this morning and at the university this afternoon.

In the temple, I meet Vrinda, a Connecticut native who is a self-defined "seeker." In her younger years, Vrinda roamed the world looking for answers. She lived in different parts of India, Europe, and Israel, and absorbed the cultures and philosophies of these different countries. To her disappointment, the first years of her journey did not yield the answers that she was hoping to find. The information seemed academic and distant, and the teachers did not always practice what they had preached.

> In the early days, what I found is that there was a big difference between what people learned and what they experienced. Going down the road of knowledge without the experience and without that love, it becomes information. And information is a funny thing when it comes to spiritual and religious thinking. It has an effect on one's ego. Having more information does not equal the true knowledge of God; in order to experience that, you have to experience it in your heart.

One of Vrinda's fundamental realizations was that personal growth occurs more through the heart and body than it does through the mind. Her travels and experimentation eventually led her to a master in India, who taught her that each individual has their own unique and special purpose.

> What my spiritual master taught me is how to love God. The innate love that we have needs to be directed toward God. It goes hand in hand with the knowledge, but the knowledge is not sufficient. Every soul longs for happiness. That desire is being translated through the mind and the senses and is filtered until you go through life endlessly seeking things that will make you happy and you consume something only to consume it again.

> Everyone is a native devotee of God, but they don't have the right information on how to obtain the happiness they are

yearning for, because the whole society is telling us, "You'll be happy if you have a family, house, car, get your body buffed, dye your hair blond." And these things will make you happy only for a limited time, because they work on the senses only and do not touch the soul. And the soul is still a beggar, and inside it is begging, longing for that thing.

The mind is like a monkey in the tree and meditation first helps you empty the mind to divorce yourself from your daily routine. When you can empty your mind, you can finally focus it, and then absorb the mind — now looking at the world through a lens of love. Once this happens, it affects daily life dramatically — it's like being in love or having a baby — your consciousness of the baby/love (God) is still there always and it changes you.

When Vrinda speaks, I recall how I felt when my daughter was born. A feeling of complete vulnerability, awe, and happiness, all at the same time and in the deepest possible sense. A feeling that is ultimate, with no constraints or dampers, like the feelings of a young child. Is this what it means to be "looking at the world through a lens of love"? If it is, then I have experienced it, and I continue to experience it each time I remember to pause and truly look at my wife and my children. I wonder if that feeling can somehow be sustained beyond the moment.

I thank Vrinda, take a few photos with her, and continue to walk in the garden around the temple. The air is still and serene, and peacocks wander around among the trees. I think of her remarkable experience. She's traveled the world and back, looking for answers that were always within her. Her mind learned the rules and concepts, but going on the road is what opened her heart. The experience.

From the Hindu temple, I head back to town to meet with Dr. Jamie Pennebaker. This morning, I learned that inner peace cannot be found in the words of others. Now, I hope to learn about the power of my own words. Pennebaker is the one who pioneered the analysis of language in psychological research. In his first experiments circa 1986, he asked college students to spend fifteen minutes writing about "the most traumatic or upsetting experiences of their entire lives." They wrote for four consecutive days, after which he continued to track their well-being and observe their health. His findings unveiled the benefits of expressive writing and gave birth to a new discipline of behavioral research; looking at people through their words.

Pennebaker also uncovered the "active ingredient" in language: putting things into a structure. Normally, our internal world is amorphous. Thoughts are mixed with feelings and emotions to form a heterogeneous soup that constantly stews in the mind. In an unsuccessful attempt to make sense of things, we often find ourselves ruminating, going in circles in a continuous "chatter in the head." On the other hand, human language is highly structured. When our thoughts and feelings are forced into molds of language, insights surface, things come to a close, and the "voice in the head" is silenced. This structuring process may be the very foundation of all modern psychotherapy.

MOST PSYCHOLOGY IS BULLSHIT

A few days ago, there was a shooting incident on the university's campus. A disturbed student brought a machine gun to class, sprayed gunfire around him, and eventually took his own life. Miraculously, all bullets missed, and the only person harmed in the event was the shooter himself. Today, the campus is vibrant and lively, showing no evidence of the shooting. It is a sunny, early fall day, and students are buzzing on the sidewalks between classes before heading into the Psychology building. Pennebaker is the chair of the department, and his office is up on the fourth floor. In his style, he is almost a stereotypical Texan, upfront and direct. At some point in our conversation, he states, "All of self-help is bullshit and probably most of psychology." He is only half-serious, but it is still an unusual statement coming from one of the most prominent psychologists of our time:

Here's my recommendation: Show me the money. Show me whatever you've got — does it work? Does it work for you? One thing I encourage everybody is to be their own inner scientist; you have to find out what's really working. I think most of the self-help work, much of positive psychology, much of all psychology, much like most religions, most of anything, is probably bullshit. It's all air. Some of the right work I think is air. You try it and afterwards — are you objectively better? Very often — not, but you have done all you can to convince yourself. My view is: try to get some objective information from yourself: are you sleeping better? Are you getting along with your family better? Are you more productive at work? Are you spending more time doing what you like? If these measures are objectively making a difference, by God — stick with them. If they stop working, try something else. Sometimes writing is helpful, sometimes it's not. For some people, it seems to be really helpful, sometimes it's not. Don't believe any of this stuff. All of these movements...and I get so pissed off by all of these movements, where there is this guru belief that this method is right, this method is truth — that is false.

Sometimes, it's right, sometimes it's not, but I would encourage everybody to try to look at it in a cold, distant way, and if it works for you — great, keep doing it.

I argue that most people are not always good at assessing how well it works for them. In response, Pennebaker suggests that people take their "life pulse" every day.

Well, then you start to measure. You start to write down how many hours of sleep you are getting. You write down how you feel today. Are you sick? What's your body temperature? There are a million ways to evaluate how your life is going. And yes, we are all delusional about things, but measuring things is not a bad idea. What's your heart rate and your blood pressure today? How many calories are you eating? How much exercise are you getting? How many fights have you gotten into with friends and coworkers? Make a list of things that are important to you — ideally, things that you can objectively measure. Take your life-pulse every day, see how it's going. And if you try something new that some-body is selling, that everybody's trying, go ahead and buy it. See if it makes a difference, and if it does, that's wonderful, and if it doesn't, get in line. Most things really don't work.

Positive Writing Isn't "Positive Thinking"

When compared with objective health data, the analysis of language can unveil what characterizes the kind of writing that yields better health and well-being. Just like Barbara Fredrickson, Pennebaker advocates positivity but warns that to falsely paint life pink is not only useless, but potentially harmful.

Over the last several years, we've done a lot of work on language analysis: what can you learn about people by the way they talk, by the way they write…if someone is being truthful or deceptive, if someone feels good or bad about themselves. We're good at knowing if they're sick or healthy, if they are a male or a female, young or old…By understanding the words people use we get a sense of how they think and how writing is influencing their thinking… We do know, for example, in writing (this is through language analysis) that people benefit more if they're more positive in their writing, so they use more positive emotion words. When they write about horrible experiences, they can still acknowledge positive things. We also know that if they've had a trauma and they're writing about it, it's important for them to acknowledge the negative sides as well. In other words, being "chipper upbeat" in dealing with bad things is not healthy. It's important to be genuine.

WRITE A NEW STORY

Writing seems to be effective in improving well-being, reducing stress, and even expediting the healing of physical wounds. But what is it about writing that makes it so effective? What are the "active ingredients" in expressive writing that lead to these positive changes? An important transformative component is *a change in perspective*. Very often, an emotional burden is not a direct result of events, but rather, comes out of the story we construct around them. Writing allows us to create a new story to replace the old one, with a perspective that is more beneficial to accept and cope with. This change in perspective is a process that lies in the basis of many methods of psychotherapy, in some Buddhist practices, and in the work of Byron Katie, who I will be meeting with in Los Angeles.

When you write, it's not as though you're throwing out the emotions. You are now thinking about the events; you are tying them together. The mere fact that you put it into words seems to make a big difference. It allows you to move past it, to move through it…Writing brings some kind of meaning and closure to events. We know that people whose health improves most are also able to change perspectives in their life. They can talk about their feelings and thoughts but also those of other people around them…We also know that in writing, it's really important that people are able to construct a story. If someone comes in and they write about a trauma, and they immediately have a good story: "this happened, and the reason was so and so"— they don't benefit from writing at all. People benefit more when they construct a new story. They start putting things together. The alternative argument is that one reason people are screwed up is because of language as well. I mean, if you look at most animals, they don't need psychotherapy, but they don't have language either to get them messed up.

"So the story is both the culprit and the solution?"

Exactly.

"Do you think riding a motorcycle is a good intervention?"

I would not do it myself. I would probably go for a ride in a nice car.

PENNEBAKER'S WISDOM:

- Be your own scientist. Be open to try new ideas and new programs, scrutinize them using objective measurements, then stick with the ones that work
- Be open and try to adapt new perspectives. Write a new story instead of the old one all over again
- Use writing to gain clarity about events in your life, their meaning, and the way you choose to respond
- Realize that the story you choose to tell determines your well-being, and you have the power to change it

PART II:
GETTING FOUND

DAY 14, OCTOBER 2ND: MESAS, BUZZARDS, AND INNER PEACE

I LEAVE AUSTIN EARLY ON RANCH ROAD 1431 AND RIDE TOWARD the Blue Bonnet Café, a famous biker hangout in Marble Falls. The sun is not quite out yet and it's a chilly Saturday morning. Austin vanishes quickly, making way for the farms of Hill Country, and the sky is painted red by the dawn. Like me, the world is now slowly awakening. A few motorcyclists pass by, dropping their left hand to wave and disturbing the silence with their rumbling engines.

An hour later, the Texas sun is up in the sky and the cold ground starts to heat. At the parking lot behind the Blue Bonnet Café, there are rows of Harleys and sport bikes. No cars. Inside, there's a celebration of goatees, pancakes, tattoos, coffee, and eggs. This is the restaurant at the end of the universe.[17]

A hundred and fifty miles later, I am on Route 190 going west toward Eldorado. I don't know much about the town, but with a name like that, I expect it to be an interesting place. The hills are gone, and the landscape changed into flat, dry sands and yellow grass, polka-dotted with small, hairy bushes. The sun is now high in the sky, and the wind is warm and comforting. Every now and then, I pass a bridge that states the name of a dry river or creek. When I eventually arrive in Eldorado, I am surprised to find a few houses, two gas stations, and a little park. Nothing more. I stop at one of the stations, go inside to get a soda, and ask the cashier for suggested things to see in town. She looks at me with a stern, serious face and says, "Nothing." "Nothing?" I ask. "This is Eldorado! There must be something interesting to see." She looks at me again trying to figure out if I am trying to make fun of her, pauses for a second, and repeats her answer, this time slowly, to make sure I understand: "N o t h i n g."

A little disappointed and baffled, I continue west, seeking some belated adventure for the day. The sun is now at its peak, pounding on the helmet. On the map, there are no towns west of here for quite some time, and indeed, over a stretch of a hundred and twenty miles, I am the only one on the road, apart from a few occasional trucks. The pavement blazes straight into the horizon, embedded in flat, dry, yellow land, spotted with a few trees, and decorated with flat-topped mesas. Every now and then, I pass a group of cows crowding underneath a single tree, seeking shelter from the scorching heat. Buzzards circle in the sky, and sometimes fly down to pick at the remains of dead animals at the side of the road. I remember watching old Western movies as a kid. When birds circled in the sky, you knew that someone was either dead or dying. The thought makes me laugh and then immediately gets me worried.

Tired, thirsty, and almost out of gas, I finally arrive in a small town called Iraan. There is one motel here, and I am debating whether to call it a day and check in. In the meantime, I fill up the motorcycle and walk into Godfather Pizza to grab a bite. The slice is excellent, and the lady who makes it tells me the story of the town and its name: This land was originally the property of ranchers Ira and Ann Yates. In 1926, they found oil here and started building what's known today as the Yates oil field. Workers started to move in, and the Ohio Oil Company built new homes to house the employees and their families. The early residents then decided to name the place Iraan, after Ira and Ann Yates.

I walk outside and look up at the sun's position. There are about two hours left before dark, enough time to carry on west to Fort Stockton. I get on the bike and go. Right before sundown, I arrive in town and check into a small, family-run motel. In its center, there's a little patio with a display of life-size statues: two cowboys and two bears, standing in the yard and keeping guard. I love Texas.

Day 15, October 3rd: A Desert Adventure, Vietnam Veterans, Fancy Junk, and Unusual Objects

I WAKE UP IN THE ROOM AND LOOK AROUND TO RECALL WHERE I AM. There is no sunlight in the small gap between the curtains and the window. It's still dark outside. I sit at the edge of the bed and try to gauge the sensations in my body, my emotions, and my thoughts. In spite of the early hour, my mind is clear, but the confinement of the room makes me feel restless. I want to get up and go. Outside, I put the motorcycle in neutral and start it up to warm the engine. It roars loudly for a second, disturbing the absolute silence of the morning, and then goes back to a quiet growl. The desert is still sleeping, covered in a dark blanket of chill. The streets are empty. The only place with the lights on is a drive-in restaurant. A woman wearing a headset is standing there in the kitchen, preparing the place for the day. I park and place my order from behind the glass, and she and I talk for a few minutes. When the food is ready, she brings it over to the table and sits next to me. She is in her fifties, short, with short brown hair. Her face is slightly wrinkled, and she speaks with a foreign accent that I cannot recognize. Our conversation drifts slowly, matching the pace of the morning and the lazy rising of the sun. With the last sip of coffee, I feel antsy again and say goodbye. I get back on the motorcycle and head out, surprised to realize that I can't remember what she and I had talked about.

As soon as the bike goes back on the highway, my restlessness is gone. The road whispers "I missed you," and I surrender to it, allowing it to carry me away. The morning air is biting cold and I can't feel my face. I continue riding for some time, until eventually I pull over and take a bandana out of the bag to tie over my mouth and nose. Now I am warmer, but the bandana constantly flaps in the wind over my eyes. I can't see a thing. For a few miles, I ride with one hand holding it down, until finally it gets untied and disappears in the wind behind me. My face feels frozen again but I'm relieved to be able to see the road. All of a sudden, a gurgle builds up in my stomach, getting stronger and stronger until it bursts out of my mouth into the cold wind. I'm surprised to hear myself laughing out loud.

Two hours later, I reach Van Horn. Next to Elm Street, there's a large yard with sculptures made of old car parts, cacti, and cattle skulls. A large sign next to it says 'Fancy Junk and Unusual Objects.' Down the road, a pink Buick with bull horns on its hood is parked in the driveway. The seats are covered with fake zebra skin. This place is fun. I stop to get lunch and look at the map. Route 54, a small side road, goes out of town, into the desert toward New Mexico. It could be an interesting alternative to El Paso and I decide to give it a shot. There is still plenty of daylight left in the day for an unplanned adventure.

The landscape on Route 54 is beautiful and iconic: flat, lunar, and spotted with large mesas. A dry, dusty wind blows in the midst of it. The motorcycle swings back and forth like a pendulum through the shallow hills, and the perception of distance becomes distorted. It feels like riding in circles. At some point, I realize that I need to calculate the amount of gas I have left in the tank. The odometer shows fifty eight miles since the last fill. Depending on where I am, I may not have enough gas to go through. I pull over to assess the situation. I haven't seen a single car since I left town. It's very hot, and I only have one small bottle of water. This is not a good place to be stuck without fuel. The map on my phone says that there's a gas station down the road, fifty miles away. The math is simple: at this speed, a full tank will get me a little over one hundred and fifty miles, so if I pass the 75th mile, I will not be able to go back. If I get to that gas station and discover that it is closed, the odometer will be at 108 miles. There wouldn't be enough gas to get to the next station and — not enough to go back. I'll be stuck in the desert. I can go back to town now to refuel, but that could take another two hours, and I will end up riding here in the dark. The risk is too high, and I decide to stick to the original plan. I head back to Van Horn, swinging in the opposite direction of the same curves, and then take I-10 toward El Paso. When the mighty mountains of Juarez become visible on the horizon, light rain starts coming down; chubby, round drops, falling one at a time. It continues for a few minutes and then stops. I am glad I decided not to ride through the desert. Adding rain to the equation would have meant slippery mud. Perhaps even a flood.

In the outskirts of El Paso, I stop to refuel and find myself at the pump next to two Harleys: A man on a Fat Boy, with a teardrop tattooed next to his eye; and a man and a woman sitting on a Street Glide. The woman has a long braid of white hair sticking out of her helmet, and her arms are covered with colorful sleeves of tattoos. The three friends are Vietnam veterans from Indiana, riding together to a reunion of The Marines in El Paso. The Fat Boy has no trunk or saddle bags, only a sissy bar with a small black plastic bag strapped to it. That is all the luggage. A seventy-year-old guy riding from Indiana to Texas and back, and everything fits in a plastic bag. He tells me about his children and about the "bug," the virus of restlessness and wanderlust that has not gone away since the war. I think about the young Marine I met back in Tennessee. It seems as though being in the service changed these guys forever. For them, riding across the country is not a single isolated trip. It's become a way of life. I wonder if that will happen to me too. Is this my first trip of many?

I pass through El Paso passively and indifferently, which surprises me. I had always been curious about this city, but I guess I have met my quota of stops for the day. I am starting to feel tired. An hour later, I arrive in Las Cruces, New Mexico. The sun is just setting. When I get off the bike in the motel parking lot, my body feels heavy, sluggish, and fatigued. It's time to give them old bones some rest. A man is standing in the parking lot smoking a cigarette. He starts a conversation, asking me if I rode all the way from New York. I respond on auto-pilot, providing premade answers and trying to end the conversation quickly. My body desperately needs to rest. In the motel lobby, I adjust my watch an hour back to Mountain Time. I am now officially in the West — on the other side of the country.

Day 16, October 4th:
The Point beyond Dreams

WHEN SOMETHING GRAND IS ABOUT TO HAPPEN, WE SPEND A LOT OF time and energy attempting to imagine it. As kids, we spent summer vacations trying to imagine the next school year. What will the teacher be like? Where in the school will the classroom be? Where will I sit? Then, when school started, we were surprised to discover how different the actual experience was. We stopped imagining, and instead, began to absorb the new reality. This process is the very essence of all personal growth. When you let go of old perceptions and make way for new realities, you move up to the next grade.

A week ago in New Orleans, I passed the point of no return: I stopped thinking about the roads behind and started thinking about the roads ahead. Waking up this morning in the West, I am beyond a deeper point in the journey — the point where a new reality takes over, and the old perception is gone: *the point beyond dreams*. My prior imagination of the *Ride* ended in Texas. I could not even imagine myself out here in New Mexico. Now, I have no prior mental image to compare with. I've moved up to the next grade. This morning, I leave Las Cruces filled with a sense of exploration and adventure like never before.

About fifty miles west on I-10, I take the exit to Route 180, toward Route 61. At the side of the road, yellow plains are stretched to the horizon, and beyond them emerge giant mountains that fade into pale blue skies. Small trees appear intermittently and every few miles a road-sign warns of rattlesnakes. None of the songs I have in my playlists fit this landscape. I turn off the music, and in my mind, play the theme song from *The Good, The Bad, and The Ugly*[18]. I look at the short, dry trees and imagine a donkey tied to one of them. A cowboy is sitting next to it, sipping whiskey straight from a dirty brown bottle, unaware of a nasty rattlesnake slithering on a rock behind him.

At a small rest stop down the road, I meet a friendly park ranger and share with him my association of whiskey, cowboys, and donkeys. He gets it and smiles, although in the decades he's been working here he's never seen any cowboys or donkeys. He does see rattlesnakes every day. He warns me to keep my eyes and ears open for the baby snakes that hatch at this time of year. Being smaller in size and not having a fully grown rattle, they are harder to spot and to hear, although they are just as dangerous as their fellow adults.

Thirty minutes later, I arrive in the City of Rocks State Park and ride slowly on the gravel paths between the unusual rock formations. Thirty million years ago, lava boiled here under the surface with a pressure that is a thousand times stronger than any volcanic activity we experience today. The lava burst through cracks in the ground and immediately cooled to form pointy rocks sticking out of the shell of the earth. In the millions of years that passed, the winds and rains continually polished the surface of the rocks and today, they look like giant river pebbles. The slow ride between these natural statues is incredible, and I constantly stop to walk around and take pictures.

After leaving the park, I take the longer way to Silver City, through Routes 61 and 152. The bike sweeps through the curves of the surprisingly Mediterranean landscape, between the hills. Different from the yellow plains of this morning, the sides of the road are sprinkled with green trees, typical of the mountainous terrain of Greece or Spain. The higher altitude is also felt in the chill of the wind that now flows through the warm air. On Route 152, small signs lead the way to the old Santa Rita copper mine. I stop the motorcycle and dismount. A few cars are parked on the gravel shoulder overlooking the open, brown pit. One of them is a large black van with a handicap permit. A man in a wheelchair is sitting next to it, gazing at the green copper craters. His thin white hair flies in the feeble wind. Without looking at me or changing his sitting position, he asks "What kind of bike is that?" He says that he used to ride when he was younger and describes his old motorcycle, a BMW 600.

The old man grew up in this region of New Mexico, moved out, lived in different places for many years and then recently returned. Throughout our conversation, he keeps his eyes on the copper mine in front of him, like a man watching a movie or driving a car. I am trying to exercise my manners and refrain from prying, but my curiosity takes over, asking one question after another. He continues to answer with his eyes glued to the mine, as if he is waiting for something to happen down there. The man is 94 years old, born in 1916. His wrinkled face is peaceful and calm and his posture is upright and erect. Before I leave, I ask him if he needs help getting back into the van. He finally turns to me, smiles, and says, "Thank you, young man, I am fine." I take one last look at him, get on the motorcycle, and ride on west toward Route 180. It could be that my encounter with this man is not an omen, a sign, or even an event of any real significance, but it left me with a spiritual, perhaps even mystical impression. This man who was born here in 1916, lived a full life and came back to the land of his childhood just before it was time to leave.

Route 180 winds through Gila National Forest, far from any town or village. The forest is dense and lush. It's hard to believe that only yesterday, I rode through the dry desert in Texas. The curves on the road are sharp and butterflies fly in my stomach as I gear-shift down and lean the motorcycle into each turn. With the increase in altitude, the air slowly gets cooler and the trees thicker and taller. I stop at the last gas station before reaching the Arizona state line, in the small village of Glenwood, and quickly continue up the road toward the mountains. Past Glenwood, the rise in elevation is rapid, climbing 1,500 feet in less than twenty minutes. The forest is now composed solely of pine trees. The chilly wind is gone, and the cold air is still. The road continues to climb through the forest, and an hour later, reaches an elevation of 8,000 feet. The engine underneath me grunts quietly, protesting both the loss of horsepower to the altitude and the demands of the constant climb. Right after crossing the Arizona line, Luna Lake appears on the right. It is beautiful and surrounded by pointy rows of pines. Who knew that Arizona could look like Switzerland? I am almost tempted to turn toward the lake, but I worry that the motorcycle will not restart if I stop it now. I continue and push through the small town of Alpine and examine the setting sun. There is about one hour left until dark. Today's final destination will be the town of Eagar, about forty minutes away. The temperatures drop further as the road continues to climb. The motorcycle follows the pull of the throttle silently and unwillingly. The views around me disappear. I stop noticing anything but the road and focus all of my energy on getting to my destination. I want to get off the motorcycle, but the road winds uphill and there's no shoulder at the side of the road and nowhere to stop. When I finally get to Eagar, I'm exhausted and freezing. I park the motorcycle, go inside, and sit in the warm motel lobby. For a few minutes, I can't speak. After carrying the bags to the second floor, I climb on the bed and lay on my back to rest. A soothing sense of relief conquers my entire body, as I lay on the bed and stare at the brush strokes of paint on the ceiling.

Day 17, October 5th: Motorcycle Service in Show Low, Tornado in Flagstaff

ARRIVING YESTERDAY IN THE TWILIGHT, TIRED AND COLD, I neglected to notice the serenity of this town. Everyone and everything in Eagar is peaceful. The presence of the forests and lakes are felt in the crisp, inviting air that flows like mist through everyone's lungs and in between the houses and shops. A full-time nomad would have stayed in Eagar for a few weeks; possibly even end his wandering and settle here. But a temporary nomad like me, with a family waiting at home, must leave this morning and move on west. My first destination is the town of Show Low, about fifty miles west on Route 60, where I called ahead yesterday to schedule a motorcycle checkup. Every morning, I check the motorcycle's brakes, oil, and tire pressure, but I've never been too skilled at the art of motorcycle maintenance. Having gone over three thousand miles now and pushing the engine to its limits yesterday, I'd like a mechanic to take a look at it, just in case.

The morning air is cold and humid and fog keeps building up inside the helmet's visor. Every few minutes, I have to pull over and use the fog spray, but to no avail. The mountain mist keeps forming inside the visor, condensing into tiny drops. Eventually, I keep the visor up and ride slowly with squinty eyes through the cold air. All around, there is nothing. Just brown dirt covered with grey fog, stretching all the way to the horizon. The carpet of fog creates an optical illusion, making the scenery seem smaller, as if the motorcycle is in a snow globe. The cold paralyzes my thoughts and my mind goes numb. All that remains now are the dirt, fog, and the cold.

Halfway to Show Low, I stop at a small gas station and enjoy the relief of standing up and stretching. The sun peeks between the clouds and the fog is slowly dissipating. Everything starts to look normal again. The station only has two pumps, dating to the 1980s with seven-segment[19] style electronic displays. One of the pumps is out of order. Inside, at the convenience store, there's a woman working behind the counter, possibly the owner. She is tall and lithe and her hair is long and dark. The expression on her face is calm and pleasant, but when she turns to me and speaks, I gather all my energy to avoid showing the repulsion at the sight of her mouth. Some of her teeth are missing and others are decayed or discolored. She smiles a big smile, as though she is not aware of it, but she must be. The contrast between the sight of her mouth and her young, friendly appearance is unbearable. Nausea hits my stomach. After paying and walking outside, I take big gulps of the crisp mountain air to recover.

By the time I arrive at the motorcycle shop in Show Low, the sun has chased all the clouds away and it is now a beautiful, early-fall day. The mechanic at the dealership greets me with the smile that is reserved for fellow bikers and checks the motorcycle from head to toe. He tests the brakes, looks at the wheel alignment, and leans down to listen closely to the breathing of the engine. His movements are slow, focused, and thorough. He examines the color of the oil on the dipstick with the face of an art critic looking at a museum painting. After checking the motorcycle, he proceeds to check the sound system and tapes the mesh on the handlebar-mounted speakers so they don't buzz when the music gets loud. Upon completion of his examination, the mechanic concludes that the bike is in great shape. He refuses to accept any payment and goes promptly back to continue his day's work. I wish him well and think of the words of the Bhagavad Gita,[20] "No one who does good work will ever come to a bad end, either here or in the world to come."

On the way from Show Low to the town of Snowflake, my heart suddenly fills with a burst of happiness. The scenery is spectacular; prehistoric mountains that open up to infinite plains. A sense of elation slowly builds and it intensifies further when signs on the side of the road lead to the famous Wigwam Motel on Route 66. After taking pictures of the iconic site to send home to the kids, I roll the bike to the restaurant opposite the motel and stop for lunch. The place is humming with the chatter of young European tourists, overflowing with the collective joy of both customers and workers. I find myself smiling for no good reason. I look around and realize that everyone else in the restaurant is smiling as well; some people are wearing a subtle smile with their lips tucked together, some exposing a shy pair of incisors, and some open wide, laughing a rolling laugh. An unfamiliar sense of calm fills every fiber in my body. I feel peaceful, complete, accepting, and loving, connected to everyone in the restaurant. No effort is required. Decisions, actions, or thoughts do not have to be made, they just naturally happen. I can leave, stay, go, talk, or be silent. It doesn't matter.

Back on the interstate, the air is no longer still, and strong, turbulent, gusts have taken over. Mighty northern winds keep pushing the motorcycle to the left lane, and when I lean and push against them, they respond with southern bursts of air, moving the motorcycle back in the other direction. In the midst of this exhaustive battle to keep the bike upright, the sky darkens to an intimidating barricade of rainclouds. At first, the rain is thin, scattering in the wind in all directions like aerosol spray. Then it thickens progressively, forming large, pear-shaped drops falling in a sharp diagonal angle, bowing to the force of the wind. The rain gradually becomes heavier and the air starts swarming with water. The front wheel cuts through the puddles, spraying the water on my thighs and my torso. The storm is now violent and persistent. Flagstaff is nearing and I can stop there for the night, but the motorcycle crawls slowly through the rain and the minutes linger. Drained and worn out, I finally see the highway exit to the right and behind it, the inviting strip of motels. I take it and gather my last bits of energy by imagining my future self, clean and dry, lying down on the motel bed. But the ride is yet to be over. Disoriented and confused by the rain and wind, only minutes from the motels, I take the wrong turn at the end of the ramp, and wind up riding away from town toward the Walnut Canyon National Monument. The road is narrow with no shoulder. There is no way to turn the motorcycle around without sliding and dropping it. I keep riding in the opposite direction of my awaited destination for a few desperate miles — a prisoner of the narrow road and the nasty weather. Three miles later, there is a little booth at the entrance to the park, and the road widens a little, allowing me to make a slow U-turn and head over to the motel. In less than five minutes, I'm there, at the reception of the Flagstaff Days Inn.

In the lobby, the TV is on and a local channel is showing the weather report. The storm that I rode through this afternoon was no ordinary storm. It was a tornado. I go back to the motorcycle and start to unload. While taking the bags off and putting them on the luggage cart, I realize that I am shaking. I pause for a second to scan my body and my emotions. I am broken with longing for Gili and the kids. When I get to the room, I sit on the bed in my wet clothes and immediately call them. On the other end of the line, our babysitter picks up and tells me that Gili went to back-to-school night. I talk with the kids and email them some pictures. A layer of quiet sadness falls on me. I miss my family.

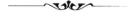

DREAMS MATTER

People I meet on the road often share their dreams with me. A nameless biker who lives four thousand miles away is a great confidant. Random conversations in gas stations, restaurants, rest areas, or hotel parking lots start with the weather and end with personal fantasies, aspirations, and regrets.

In a small town in North Carolina, nestled in the Blue Ridge Mountains, I met a hotel receptionist. A smart and interesting young man who is designing a Dungeons and Dragons game with a new and complex system of rules. I could tell by the way he speaks that he is completely immersed in his project, radiating with excitement and joy. In Tuscaloosa Alabama, I spent an hour speaking with the gas station attendant. He works at a gas station to save for college so that he can become a teacher, the first step toward becoming an author. The list of dreams is endless: visit a close relative who lives far away, start a business, go to Japan, learn a second language.

And of course, with age, the syntax changes. "I will" and "I am" becomes "I wanted to" and "I should have." To me, this is the heart of the midlife challenge. Midlife is the point in time when people tend to put their dreams to rest, expecting peace and acceptance, not realizing that abandoned dreams continue to boil like lava under a thin surface. I think that dreams are meant to be pursued, not accomplished. To flourish and to experience life to its full capacity, a person needs to be engaged in the pursuit of his or her dreams every day. The active quest matters much more than the accomplishment.

In the turbulence of daily life, we are all drowning in deadlines, obligations, carpools, tasks, and chores. These are important. Without them, we would not have the things we need and value: a roof over our heads, safety, and a good education for our children. But our dreams matter too, and in the absence of external pressure to chase them, they are often abandoned and die. A year ago, I did not have a motorcycle license and never even sat on a motorcycle before. Now, I am in Arizona after riding four thousand miles from home. One thing led to another. You never know.

DAY 18, OCTOBER 6TH: RAINBOWS OVER THE GRAND CANYON

THE LOBBY IS BUZZING WITH PEOPLE HAVING BREAKFAST AND chatting. No one pays attention to the television. Flagstaff is the closest town to the Grand Canyon and all of the motel guests are excited about their day, anticipating their visit to this miracle of nature. I get some coffee and sit down in front of the TV. The forecast for the day includes rain, wind, and thunderstorms. A tornado alert is still in effect. Yesterday's storm caused significant property damage and a freight train was derailed by the wind. My heart cringes at the realization of the danger I was in. I imagine the bike being slammed to the ditch at the side of the road, sliding and falling. I imagine being hurt and waiting for help in the rain, the call from the hospital, Gili visiting me, the flight back home together a few weeks later. My heart cringes. The storm hit so unexpectedly yesterday. Did I really put myself in such danger?

I was planning to check-out this morning, ride to the Grand Canyon, and head on west, but after listening to the news, I decide to leave my stuff in the motel, stay an additional night, and go on a guided tour. Having traveled alone for more than two weeks now, I look forward to the company of others, even if it means deviating from the heroic easy-rider storyline. Fifteen minutes later, I am in a van with ten other tourists, sitting next to a couple from Laurel, Mississippi. The husband's southern accent is smooth and reassuring; he practically sings the words into sentences. His words go up and down like music. I was just in Laurel last week, and it is interesting to talk to them about their hometown. I thought that Laurel was calm. The girls working at the Laurel Pizza buffet said it was boring. The couple in the van say that it's a great place to raise kids. It makes a lot of sense and reminds me of my home in the suburbs, safe, calm, but perhaps a tad boring. As the youngest person in the van, I am immediately labeled by the group as "the kid," and become collectively adopted. I am relieved to be safe, warm, taken care of, guided, and passive. The van reminds me of a school bus, and it's a school trip at the end of the school year with no homework or exams to worry about.

Climbing up toward the Grand Canyon, the weather gets worse. Trees are flattened by the wind, and white chunks of hail the size of tennis balls fall from the sky. They remain on the ground and pad the side of the road, providing an insane testimony to the brutality of the weather. Two guys on Harleys ride in front of us. They're sitting stiff in the motorcycle seats, trying to stay focused as the hail hits them. The driver keeps a safe distance from them. I listen to the tour guide's explanations and feel happy and proud that I kept my promise to my wife to stay safe.

In the hours that follow, the weather lightens up, and a weak sun sends rays through the mist. The result is an array of multiple, full rainbows beneath us, inside the canyon. It is magnificent to be standing above the rainbows and looking down at them. They look like man-made optical illusions. A biblical vision, like an omen designed to show the presence of the Divine to the doubters. I feel humbled and grateful for the opportunity to see it. I am grateful for the clouds, for the rain, and for the storm.

DAY 19, OCTOBER 7TH: ENLIGHTENMENT ON ROUTE 66

EVERYTHING FLOWS. THE MOUNTAINS, SUN, RAIN, AND CLOUDS all flow easily, moving at a pace that is just above noticeable. Accurately, in a quiet, oscillating rhythm. In slow motion. In the midst of all of it, the motorcycle rolls instinctively, dancing with the air to the beat of the wind, caressing the mountain through the pavement, buzzing like a small insect flying in the hive of nature. All attempts are gone. No thought is needed. The motorcycle runs by itself and the roads unfold and gradually reveal the way. We flow effortlessly through all of it, in sync with the random movement of the clouds, the arbitrary gusts of wind, and the slower but certain movement of the earth. There is no destination, no route, and no origin. All I do is let go and let the motorcycle flow naturally in the spaghetti of objects, particles, and energy that is the world. It is all in me. The mountains, swarming with animals; the depth of the oceans; the forests, flowing to the movement of the wind. All falling leaves, laughing children, ants rebuilding their nests after the storm, cars, mushrooms, teapots, buildings, airplanes, chairs, ridges, continents. It is all in me. Vast and uncontainable, unless I let go and simply let it flow, do its own dance, without trying to alter it in any way.

My breath is the air; the rubber is the asphalt. I am the motorcycle. I am the mountains. I am the sun, the clouds, and the rain. I am the road.

I am the road.

*   *   *

Westbound on Interstate 40, gusts of wind keep pounding at the motorcycle from the left, trying to push it off the road, just like they derailed the freight train two days ago. Luckily, the winds are now too weak to turn the motorcycle over, but each gust still thrusts us a few yards to the right. I end up riding on the left side of the right lane, keeping a safe distance from the ditch at the side of the road as the wind pushes me time and again to the shoulder. Close to Bellemont, on the other side of the highway, right past the Grand Canyon Harley Davidson dealership, there's a parking lot with a few dozen large RVs. I turn my head left to look at it. The sight is unreal. The RVs are laying sideways, wallowing in a coat of shattered glass. These massive structures of metal, laid down and spread out like little white playing cards, more evidence of the violence of yesterday's wind.

Less than an hour later, the wind finally reconciles and loses interest. Exit 146 takes me off the interstate toward Ash Fork — first on a ramp running parallel to the interstate, and then slowly departing from it onto historic Route 66. I stop for gas on Lewis Avenue, and in the parking lot, I spot an old Packard[21]. The car reminds me of my dad's old white Studebaker Lark, a shy compact sister to the luxury Packard, but still a great source of pride in Israel in the seventies. As a kid, I used every opportunity to brag about our car's leather seats and its huge front grill. It was a piece of the distant American dream, parked right outside. Even though it is old, the Packard here in the parking lot is beautiful. Its shiny ivory skin matches the classic whitewall wheels, and the chrome swan ornament still stands proudly on the tip of its hood. Walking around it, wearing the padded jacket, makes me feel like a time traveler who came from the future to visit the late fifties. In its time, this car must have ridden to beaches, parks, and forests, and was home to late-night kisses, family feuds, romantic arguments, and silent, solitary rides. It was admired, bragged about, cared for, and then eventually abandoned. For the past fifty years, it rode hundreds of thousands of miles through the roads of America, and now, it is resting in a gas station, off the interstate in Ash Fork. I look at it, mesmerized. This, here, is the Route 66 that I've been waiting for. I get back on the motorcycle, fire it up, and take a right turn down the road onto Crookton Road, to dive into the depth of historic Route 66.

The first stretch of road is about seventeen miles long, straight, and slices through planes of yellow grass, leading into the town of Seligman. A welcoming crisp breeze flows through the mesh fabric of my jacket, contrasting the growing warmth of the sun. Small, thick green trees spot the grass. There is no house, building, or another road in sight, only 360 degrees of yellow plains split by a black line of pavement and covered by a dome of sapphire sky.

On the side of the road, a little brown sign is nearing. As it gets close, I see white letters on it that say: '*T'would be nice.*' Odd. Is this a commercial of some sort? What is it about? A quarter mile later, another sign says '*to go by air.*' It appears that the brown signs are telling a story. I'm curious. All of a sudden, someone else's presence is felt here, in the yellow plains. I'm no longer alone. Someone sought to make a little game to make this straight stretch of road a little more interesting. I'm intrigued and pull the throttle to get faster to the next sign. There are four signs altogether. They read:

> '*T'would be more fun*'
> '*to go by air*'
> '*if we could put*'
> '*these signs up there*'

And then, a fifth sign says '*Burma Shave.*' I've never heard of that brand of shaving products before, but it definitely got my attention. I find myself smiling, almost laughing out loud. These signs must have been posted a while back. I'm almost tempted to pull over and use my phone to search for more information about it, but that would ruin the experience. I wish there would be signs like that all over the country. Seems like a great way to pull children's attention to the sights of the journey and away from the destination. Less asking "are we there yet?"

The road quickly reaches a chain of hills and starts to curve. At the top, the ground is rocky and a small sign says '*elevation 5700.*' Then the road becomes straight again, with the same vast plains of yellow grass from end to end. Occasionally, there's a gate to a ranch at the side of the road with a few cows standing around and grazing.

Riding on, I see another set of brown signs coming. These ones read:

> '*He tried to cross*'
> '*As fast train neared*'
> '*Death didn't draft him*'
> '*He volunteered*'
> And again: '*Burma Shave*'

The presence of the person who wrote the signs is still felt here, only now it is clear that he or she is a ghost of the past. The language and rhymes fit the era that this road represents. A road that leads to drive-ins, shaving brushes, Studebakers and Packards, and to the birth of Rock 'N' Roll. There's no better vessel to sail this river than a motorcycle. More signs follow, and after thirty minutes of roadside entertainment, I arrive in Seligman. I will see many more of these Burma Shave poems riding through Route 66 throughout the day.

In the center of Seligman stands Delgadillo's Snow Cap drive-in, a family-owned burger place that has been serving the town's visitors for almost sixty years. The 1936 Chevrolet of the first owner, Juan Delgadillo, is still parked in the front. The signs on top of the door say that the place offers burgers and 'dead chicken,' next to another sign saying 'Sorry, we're open.' The cashier and waiters play pranks on the customers. In between the jokes that are posted on the walls, below the drive-in window, hides a sign quoting President Woodrow Wilson. This one is not intended to be funny:

> '*There is no higher religion*
> *than human service. To*
> *work for the common*
> *good is the greatest*
> *CREED*'

I read it again, slower this time, and a strange feeling floods my abdomen:

> '*There is no higher religion than human service.*
> *To work for the common good is the greatest creed.*'

Man seeks meaning on a motorcycle ride and finds it on the wall of a burger joint in Arizona. Reflecting on the past three weeks, I realize this is the heart of my personal transformation. Being alone on the road, I frequently need the help of others (directions, info, change), and I've become strongly aware that others need my help too. I am constantly on the lookout for opportunities to give my assistance, my time, or my modest donation. I put a bill in every donation jar I see, whether it's for the local little league or cancer research. I give money to beggars. I stop by each car that I see on the side of the road. This behavior does not feel altruistic or notable in any way. It's become automatic. Thinking about it in terms of "giving" feels odd — you can only give what is yours, and I no longer feel that my money, time, or skills are my own. It's as if they were entrusted to me to keep and use, but they actually belong to anyone who truly needs them. I look at the sign again and decide to live the remainder of my life guided by Wilson's words and to keep the service of others as my creed.

A bunch of motorcycles is parked outside the Snow Cap. Everyone is from everywhere, and everyone is far from home. They all travel in small groups. I'm the only one here traveling alone, and it makes me feel both lonely and proud at the same time. A couple of older guys on BMW motorcycles open up a map and show me the route they are planning on taking going west. They suggest Route 93 to Vegas and then riding through Death Valley toward California. I'm lucky to have met them. In the past few days, I've been neglecting to dig in the maps. There's a good chance I would have missed it.

It's time to ride on. Route 66 between Seligman and Kingman is a hundred-mile stretch of beautiful, tranquil road that strays far from the Interstate into equanimity. Gentle curves in the road swing the motorcycle back and forth like a napping baby, relaxing to a lullaby of Burma Shave poems. I stop for a quick lunch in Peach Springs, get back on the bike, and without even noticing it, I'm already in Kingman, looking for a place to spend the night. After checking in, I call home and speak with the kids and Gili. Her voice sounds cracked. She is collapsing under the burden of chores, pick-ups, and drop-offs, and, at the same time, dealing with the coming opening of her new store. She clearly underestimated how hard it would be to do all of this on her own. Now, it's too late to turn back. I feel worried and helpless. All I can do is try to give her some advice, but I am probably the last person whose advice she would take now. After all, my ride is the source of her problem. So, I don't say anything. After hanging up, I go through my evening routine mechanically, trying hard not to sink into guilt.

*   *   *

THE POWER WITHIN

Later at night, I sit in the hotel lobby and read, trying to forget the burden that sits on my mind. When I finally manage to focus on the pages of John Steinbeck's *Travels with Charlie*, a voice next to me abruptly pulls me back to Arizona: "Interesting book?" A man with grey hair, slightly older than I am, is standing next to me. His face seems pleasant and friendly. I'm in no mood for company, so without looking at him, I say: "Yeah, it's pretty interesting," but he doesn't go away. Pretending to be immersed in reading, I can sense his presence standing next to me, transmitting an all-too-familiar vibe, the vibe of a lonely traveler. Perhaps, it's time to remember my creed. The person next to me may need my help. And most likely, I need his company as much as he needs mine.

His name is Steve Waller and he is a biochemist turned archeologist. In the past few years, he's been studying the wall art of ancient caves. He traveled to different parts of the world and looked at the cave paintings of various cultures. Using sonar-like equipment, he analyzed the acoustic properties of the spots in the caves where ancient artists chose to work. It turns out that in most cases, cave art was done in the places where the echo in the cave is the loudest. This initially may sound esoteric, but it has substantial implications about the way ancient people perceived the spirits, or God. In Native American tribes, as well as tribes in Africa and Australia, echoes were thought to be the voice of the spirits speaking from within the rock. Sometimes, they were echoes of thunderstorms or winds, but often, they were actually echoes of the cave-dwellers themselves. What they thought to be the voice of the divine was actually their own voice echoing back at them after being reflected from the surface of the rock.

We sit in the hotel lobby and have a beer, and as he describes his research work, I keep thinking how brilliant his findings are: what we perceive to be extraordinary, unexplained, and miraculous, is actually the echo of our own voice. The power is all within. Just like the participants of Pennebaker's studies who were able to expedite the healing of their physical wounds. It was not a miracle; it was them, simply resolving to heal faster and utilizing their inherent human capabilities to do just that.

Steve and I say goodbye, and I continue to sit in the lobby and reflect on the earlier phone call with home. It was probably wise to spare my wife my useless advice. She already has a fortress of power within her. All I need to do is give her the support she needs to unlock it. I feel grateful for Steve's unexpected appearance in the hotel lobby and embarrassed by my earlier testiness. The cloud of worry that's been circling around my head all evening finally goes away. I go back to my room, turn off the light, and sleep like a baby, swinging to the rhythm of the curves of Route 66.

Day 20, October 8th: Vegas Baby!

STILL IN BED AND FILLED WITH ENERGY, CLARITY, AND RESOLUTION, I decide to call home right away. Gili picks up the phone, and I immediately sense the crisis in her voice. She went to bed late last night and just got back from the morning carpool, exhausted and overwhelmed. Out of a desire to help, I start preaching my advice. "Why don't you ask our neighbor for more help?" "Perhaps you can postpone the opening of the store?" As expected, this only gets her more upset, and the call does not end up the way I had hoped. By the time I get out of bed, the high spirit is gone, but the sense of clarity remains: I understand exactly what happened, what I've done wrong, and what can be done differently. The morning routine continues sluggishly, with guilt chained to my ankle like a ball and chain.

Thirty minutes after taking off, I'm on Route 93 heading north toward Vegas, enjoying the friendly hum of the engine and surrounded by the familiar sight of the desert. Yellow dirt plains, lunar hills, and an infinite row of old wooden posts carrying power lines. Midway through Route 93, I stop for gas and go into the convenience store to buy cigarettes. I stand alongside the motorcycle and light up my loot, blowing some smoke and enjoying the scene I am in. It is so perfect that I just have to play along with it. Halfway through burning the paper-wrapped tobacco, I fire up the bike next to me in neutral and put on a heavy metal song, Saxon's "Crusader." The music starts with a prelude of melodic acoustic guitars, setting up the stage for the coming entrance of drums and distortion. I wait, and at the very precise moment, put out the cigarette, mount the motorcycle, and shift it into gear. The drums roll in as the motorcycle swerves out of the gas station and onto the highway, starting to cruise steadily to the sound of screaming vocals: "*Crusader, crusader, please take me with you...*" I lean back and press my back against the passenger bag, stretch my feet forward to the very edge of the floorboards, and take my left hand off the handlebars. I know that I'm putting on a childish show for no audience to watch, but I don't care. This is my dream, and that's how it goes, complete with metal music, a yellow desert, and tumbleweeds. It is high-noon now on Route 93 and I am a cowboy riding my horse of steel in the Arizona desert. I take a deep breath, taste the bitterness of the dirt in my mouth, and let the dry wind penetrate my chest and go into my guts. I may be putting on a show, but there are no props and no pre-written scripts. This right here is the real, tangible world.

Just before reaching the Hoover Dam, local police have placed road blockades, stopping each vehicle going north and taking a quick peek inside. The heat is heavy and the traffic is almost at a standstill. After some time of stop-and-go that feels like forever, I finally get to the policemen and stop for a second. They look at me briefly and give me a sign to continue. One always wonders what they are looking for. I pass them and pull over at a small parking lot overlooking the dam, dismount, walk around, cool off, stretch, and contemplate the plans for the day. I also call Gili and I am relieved to find that she sounds calmer and in a good mood (in a few weeks, when I am back home, she will tell me how worried she was for me, riding all by myself, much more than she was worried about her busy schedule). Two couples in a van next to me start up a conversation and inquire about my motorcycle, my trip, and my plans. They are fellow riders, about my age, and speak in the laid-back tone of cross-country travelers. The taller guy, in dark shades and a colorful t-shirt, asks if I am planning to take the Hoover Dam tour. I wasn't even contemplating it. Doing something that touristic doesn't sit well with the easy-rider fantasy I was living only thirty minutes ago. He looks at me and says "If you've never done it, you have to. You don't know what you'd be missing." While on the road, I learned to listen to the advice of veteran travelers. I feel a little guilty going sight-seeing without my family, but I follow his advice. He was obviously right. The "dam tour," as the tour-guides call it, is fascinating.

After passing the Hoover Dam, the road starts to widen and the city of Las Vegas appears in the distance. The vast desert is gone and makes way for the urban, human-inhabited part of the planet. The side of the road is sprinkled with gas stations and fast food restaurants. The only things left of the desert are the brush strokes of white clouds in the faint sky, the same sky watching over Route 93. In Vegas, I ride straight to the Luxor hotel at the south end of the strip. It's strange to be back in civilization. For the first time since leaving home, I use the chain-lock to secure the bags to the back of the bike and lock the zippers with little padlocks. I stand in the large, multi-floor parking lot, gaze at the army of parked cars, and feel the loneliness spread in the air like a drop of ink in a glass of water. None of this is real. The dividers among people, the chain-locks that guard the property of individuals, the concrete dividers on the freeway, and the white lines on the pavement, marking individual parking spots. All of these lines are imaginary. The real world outside of here is connected. It's one. I've seen it.

Crowds of people are walking around the hotel. Eight years ago, I came here with my family. I was here for a conference and Gili joined me, together with Dana and Tomer, who was still a baby. Ori, my youngest, was not yet born. We had moved to the country only a couple of years before and we still felt like tourists, discovering America. I remember how young I felt back then, and it makes me realize how much older I feel now. I step aside to light a cigarette and enjoy the forbidden pleasure of smoking indoors. Then I get some food and use my phone to look for a place to stay. I find a room on the 21st floor of the Riviera Hotel and get there just in time to stand by the window and stare at the sun setting in the mountains. At night, I go down and walk through the strip, go into a bar, gamble a little, smoke another cigarette, and drink some whiskey. I go through the motions robotically, feeling phony. I am lost. Restless again. I know that my wife's life at home is out of balance, and it deprives me of my peace. What happened to my personal transformation?

Day 21, October 9th: From Death Valley to the Promised Land

Yesterday, when I spoke with my daughter, she told me I should listen to Katy Perry's song "Waking Up in Vegas." "You'll be actually waking up in Vegas", she said, "so it will be for real." Her voice sounded excited and proud. My pre-teen daughter thinks I'm cool. That alone was worth the trip. Riding now through the empty streets of Saturday morning in Las Vegas, I keep my promise to her and play the song in full volume. Perry's voice disturbs the silence, singing "that's what you get for waking up in Vegas," scolding everyone for gambling and drinking, at least the few who are awake. In twenty minutes, I'm in the outskirts of the city on Route 95, and again, find myself wrapped in the kind arms of the desert. The road goes through a sparse forest of goofy, thin cacti, bathing in the quiet, warm rays of the sun. I am happy. I feel complete again. Inner peace, I make a quick note-to-self, is not a permanent state. A rider through life can develop the skills to obtain it, but one cannot hold onto it all of the time.

The ride is smooth, and everyone on the road drives slowly, as if they're not yet fully awake, squinting at the road with puffy eyes. I pass two guys riding brand new Fat Boys and wave at them. They both ride at a low, constant speed, bent down on the handlebars to minimize wind resistance. They lift their left hands from the grips slowly to wave back, while keeping their eyes on the road. I'm curious about this couple. It's unusual to see novice riders on big Harleys, especially all the way out here. I ride on for another thirty miles, deeper into the desert, celebrating the liberation from the confinement of the city, and then stop for gas at Indian Springs. To a lone rider, gas stations are not only a source of gasoline. They are oases, providing fuel for the body, the mind, and sometimes for the soul. Any gas station can offer quick gas, a dirty bathroom, or stale coffee. But the good stations are large, clean, and host a convenience store that is loaded with the things you really need: fresh coffee, medicine, and a warm lunch. More importantly, good gas stations offer the company of experienced fellow travelers. They hang out in the corners of the parking lot, separated from the rush of the pumps, lingering a bit to fuel their minds and their souls.

The gas station in Indian Springs is a good one. The parking lot is large and full of people walking between cars and motorcycles. The convenience store is large and clean, and a 24-hour casino accommodates gamblers who seek a final shot at the jackpot. After I finish fueling, I see the two Fat Boys pulling in. It turns out that they are college students from Germany on their summer break, touring the western United States. Their tan, smiling faces are absorbed with the sites they've seen and the roads they have traveled in the past couple of weeks. We stand around and talk for a while, exchange travel plans, stories, and ideas. When I get back to my motorcycle, I see Two Can-Am Spyders[22] parked in the corner of the parking lot. Next to them stand two men in their mid-sixties, with grey hair and radiant smiles. They are close friends who have been riding motorcycles together for years and recently traded their passion for two wheels for the three wheels of the Can-Am. The conversation starts with the inevitable discussion of storage space, reliability, and road grip, and then goes into the deeper aspects of the riding experience. "You can't describe it in words," one of them says, "Our wives and kids are worried about our safety, but they also know the good that it brings into our lives, how it changes a man for the better." A few minutes later, they mount their three-legged beasts and disappear. I stay in the corner of the parking lot for a few minutes to fuel my soul with the essence of the place and then hop on the motorcycle and head north toward Death Valley.

Beatty, the entrance point to Death Valley, is a small Wild West town that was founded during the gold rush. The "Death Valley Fire Pit BBQ" is situated right on Main St, in an old gas station. Inside, a couple dozen tourists are sitting and having lunch. The windows are small, and in spite of the strong sunlight outside, the place is dark, like a Western saloon. Two young women from Spain sit at a table near me. One of them is showing the other photos on the back of a digital camera. I hear some German in the air too, and at least one additional language that I cannot recognize. Everyone is waiting to board a car or motorcycle and go into Death Valley. The waitress scans my clothes and identifies me as a biker. "You're going into the mountains — right?" I smile and respond with a big, enthusiastic "Yes!" She keeps a serious face on and says, "Be careful." Her comment makes my blood run cold. I didn't think that this would be a dangerous ride. She notices the surprise in my face, leans a little closer, and this time with a comforting smile says, "It's okay just be a little careful."

I ride toward the slowly-nearing mountains and feel a lump of anticipation stuck in my throat as the last mark of civilization disappears from the rear-view mirrors. In the past seven days, I've grown attached to the desert; to its calm, its mystery, and its wisdom. When you ride through the desert roads, the steamy wind oozes in under your skin, and the monotone rhythm of the air adjusts your internal clock to slow motion. Death Valley turns out to be the mother of all deserts. It wraps around you from all directions and slowly levitates you to a still state of meditation. Starting at an elevation of 5,000 feet, through giant mountains, the road goes down into a flat ocean of sand dunes, and then into infinite fields of alien-looking cacti. Around the tiny village of Stovepipe Wells, the road settles to sea level and then eventually climbs up again, looping up at the edge of an abyss. Some parts of the ride are challenging, but I keep it slow and steady before entering each curve, so that the motorcycle doesn't lean in too far. The entire time, I have the helmet camera on and I keep looking sideways, not to miss a single shot of this miraculous place. It's hard to believe that this here is earth. The same planet where millions of people are now running Saturday errands, mowing their lawns, driving their kids to activities, or hanging out with friends, completely unaware of this insane scenery.

After riding for a couple of hours, I stop at the Panamint Springs gas station to fill up and to allow my brain to catch up with my eyes. Again, it hits me. I got a motorcycle license; I own a motorcycle. I left home three weeks ago and rode all the way from New York to this place, outside of earth. When I was growing up in the suburbs of Tel Aviv, the longest trip one could make before hitting the border was to the town of Eilat — two hundred miles south. I now ride that same distance each day. I have to ask myself: If all of this is possible, what else could be possible? What else awaits on the road if I decide to make it happen? I look around at the extraterrestrial landscape and vow to remember this moment. To never forget this awakening, to never go back to being dormant again.

*   *   *

The desert ends in an instant on Route 295. The trees at the side of the road are lush and green, and the ground is dark and fertile. Just before entering Lone Pine, the snow-covered peaks of the Sierra Nevada Mountains appear behind the hills, blushing in the shadows of the setting sun. In the distance stands Mt. Whitney, proud and tall, the highest point of elevation in the contiguous United States. The air smells of new possibilities, new roads, and new frontiers. This is the Promised Land, waiting at the end of a journey through the desert.

On Lone Pine's Main Street, cowboys walk around wearing saddle-fringe gloves and low hanging holsters, and riders on horses trot between passing cars. I check into a small motel, and after finishing to unpack, take a dip in the small motel pool. The sun has already disappeared behind the snowy summits, but the air is still warm from the passing day. The cool water floods my body with relief, and I close my eyes and give in to it. Later, in town, I sit next to a group of three families in the patio of the Totem Café. When they receive their food, they stop talking, hold hands, and wait for the oldest man to say grace: "We thank you, our lord, Jesus Christ, for the meal we are having this evening, and we thank you for having Chris and Heather, and Michael and Sara here with us, along with their families. We thank you for a good year in business and for the rain and the seasons that help our crops grow and bring food to our table each day. Amen."

PART III:
GETTING THERE

DAY 22, OCTOBER 10TH: YOSEMITE

AN UNFAMILIAR FEELING SCATTERS THROUGH MY BODY WHILE riding in the crisp air this morning. I am in awe of the wealth of nature, lit up by the diversity of color, and enchanted by the smell of the wind. A voice in my head announces, "You have arrived." California is not another path — it is a destination. Route 395 meanders at a corridor between the Sierra Nevada range and the Inyo Mountains. The motorcycle rides on it quietly, respectfully, dwarfing in the shadows of the savage crests. I stop at a good gas station in Bishop and enjoy the wide aisles at the large convenience store. A weekend biker holding a map is standing in the corner next to a BMW 1200, glad to share his experience of riding through Yosemite. He tells me that I am in for a treat. It snowed in the park a few days ago and the park is now covered in white. He also mentions that there is no cell phone reception once you enter the park, so I should make calls right outside, at Lee Vining. North of Bishop, the earth starts climbing up sharply, rising 2,000 feet in the course of the next twenty miles. I pull over to put on more clothes and thicken the jacket with a lining. My face is freezing, but the full-face helmet is buried in the back and I am too lazy to unstrap the bags. I wish I hadn't lost my face bandana back in Texas. Twenty minutes later, the elevation climbs another 2,000 feet and hits 8,000. I am inside the mountains now, leaning stiff on the handlebars, and battling the chill of the wind.

At Lee Vining, right outside of Yosemite, I stop at a gas station to call home and let Gili know that I will have no signal. I get some fresh coffee and walk around before calling. The warm liquid goes down slowly and spreads in my frozen torso like drain opener. It revives the stiff muscles and pushes the hesitant blood to run. I am grateful for it. Gili's voice on the other side of the line is dry and almost sounds unfamiliar. As she speaks, the core inside of me crumbles to pieces. I miss her. For the first time in the sixteen years since we've met, I cannot be there for her. We talk for a long time, alternating between peaks of love and valleys of silence. I feel helpless. All I can think of is how fortunate I am to have her support and how unworthy of it I feel right now. When I get back on the motorcycle, my limbs feel enervated and a chunk of guilt is implanted in my chest.

Immediately after turning onto Route 120, a new universe is revealed. A carpet of pines rises from the bed of snow on the sides of the hills. It cradles a lake that mirrors a painted blue sky with perfectly shaped clouds. In my entire life, never, in any place I've visited, have I seen scenery so rich. My eyes are devouring the view and slowly push away the unrest that perturbs my mind. I know this: In two weeks, when I return home, things will completely transform for the better. A tide of positive change will sweep my family, my life, and my surroundings in ways that I have yet to understand. It will pay off.

Ten minutes after entering Route 120, I spot a segment of the road with a broader shoulder and pull over to walk around a bit. I kneel down and take a picture of the motorcycle on the asphalt with the background décor of the peaks. The photo will later become the cover page of the journey and this book. I get back on the road and continue on west. Time flies by. The road climbs up another three thousand miles but now I'm oblivious to the cold. The landscape is transcendent, too beautiful to contain or process. Groups of motor-cycle riders flock the road and wave as they pass through. We are all bewitched, hypnotized.

Approaching the park exit, hours later, the elevation is down by 8,000 feet. The snow is gone and the world is back to its familiar form. The air is warm and full of flying insects that crash on the windshield and my goggles, making it hard to see the road. After riding through a cloud of bugs, I notice a disturbing buzz in my ear. I cautiously reach with my hand and pull out a live bee. Luckily, the insect is disoriented from the hit and doesn't sting. A few more miles west, I stop at PJ's café right outside of Groveland. I get off the motorcycle, pour some water on the goggles to wash off the insects, and shake my jacket. A rain of dead little creatures falls out of it.

After drinking the rest of the water in the bottle, I ride straight into town. The driveway into the Groveland Hotel's parking lot borders the Iron Door Saloon, the oldest saloon in California. It is Happy Hour now and a bunch of people are standing outside the place, enjoying the setting sun and some loud music. As I ride in through the driveway, they scream and cheer, shouting at me to come in and share a drink. They are the unofficial welcome reception of bikers. I wave back and feel like I am on top of the world, but I've got to wind down and relax. My body is weary and my mind is overwhelmed. I park the motorcycle in the back of the hotel and have to make three trips to carry the bags to my room, climbing several flights of stairs each time. When I'm finally done, I am drenched in sweat. Cell phone reception is sparse, but one of my phones works. I call Gili, hoping to hear a change in her voice. She sounds much better and she cheers me up. The sound of her voice fills me with joy. Later at night, I go to the Iron Door and order my traditional shot of Jack. The Happy Hour partygoers are gone, and a local band is playing classic rock music. Everyone, including the band, is watching a baseball game on a number of large-screen TVs. I cannot find a comfortable spot or position to sit or stand. The baseball team on TV hits a home run and everyone cheers. I can't recognize which team it is. I'm a foreigner, a stranger in a strange land. I miss New York. I miss my wife. I miss my kids. I miss the Yankees. I go back to my room and immediately fall into a bottomless sleep.

Day 23, October 11th:
Arriving in San Francisco

I WAKE UP ON A TALL BED AND SCAN the room. THE YELLOW WALLS
are decked with framed artwork and the windows are covered with
heavy drapes. A brown teddy bear is sitting on the window sill, staring outside. I haul the bags downstairs, wipe the pellets of dew from
the motorcycle seat, warm up the engine, and take off. The night
chill is still in the air, smelling like yesterday's summits. The iron
door, after which the saloon is named, is now tightly shut. Very few
cars are on the road, and the streets are empty. The morning wraps
me in a familiar blanket of calm. My mind is devoid of thoughts.
Even the recognition that today I will be reaching the Pacific Ocean
doesn't sink in. The open road and the morning air are all there is.

Just outside of Groveland, I turn onto Old Priest Grade on GPS
orders. At the side of the road, a small yellow sign says 'steep — use
low gears.' Nothing about this sign conveys danger. No exclamation
points, no bold letters, no red print. But the flat road quickly turns
into a twisty drop, descending 2,000 feet in only two miles at the
edge of a mountain. Nothing in my riding experience could have
prepared me for this dangerous dive. Surprised at my lack of anxiety,
I feather my foot on the brake, empty my mind, and gather all of my
energy to focus on the tight blind corners, trying not to think about
the chasm to my right and the car tailgating at my rear (disturbing

thought: at least if I fall off the cliff, they will call for help). The road is so steep that I can feel the excessive force of gravity literally pulling the front wheel, nose down. I have to make an effort to pull my chin up so I can see the road. Finally, the pavement straightens up and flattens alongside the Don Pedro reservoir. I can take a deep breath of relief and enjoy the sight of the glittering water. The entire episode lasted only fifteen minutes.

Three hours later, the country roads widen into massive freeways and I enter the Bay Bridge. San Francisco unfolds like a panoramic postcard: Treasure Island, the Coit Tower, Alcatraz, the Transamerica Pyramid, and the Golden Gate Bridge, all in a single frame. A year after sitting on a motorcycle for the first time (in the motorcycle safety course, which I failed), I rode solo from the Atlantic to the Pacific. I rode through the Appalachian Mountains, the Sierra Nevada, the Grand Canyon, Route 66, New Orleans, the Atchafalaya swamp... and now, I'm in San Francisco. I ride on the Embarcadero and can't believe I'm here. I made it. It's just like I dreamt, only better. Whatever comes next, I am ready for it. I rode the United States from coast to coast.

PART IV:
BEING THERE

Day 24, October 12th: The Day After

MOVIES NEVER SHOW THE DAY AFTER. THE DAY AFTER D-DAY, THE day after the family is reunited, after the finish line. The day after is always a boring day. Twenty-four hours of heavenly boredom. All I need to do is bask in the glow of my accomplishment, and prolong this moment of victory a little longer.

This morning, there is no need to pack and no need to plan. I go downstairs, grab an apple at the reception, and walk down to Pat's Café across the street. The motorcycle is parked outside the Columbus Motor Inn. Quiet, like a horse resting outside a saloon. I cross the street in my pajamas, carrying a book under my arm and taking a bite of the apple. The coy San Francisco sun is out, up in the sky. Everything feels so Sunday morning that for a moment, I forget it is actually Tuesday. People think that nomads fail to develop a sense of connection with the places they visit. The opposite is true. While on the road, nomads develop the capacity to connect immediately with a new place, as if they've lived there forever. I sit in the sun, sip my coffee, read my book, and feel that I belong here. Like I've lived here my entire life.

A few hours later, my fingers start to get antsy. I need to grip on the handlebars. I put a bandana on my head and an adventurous smile on my face and go out to ride. In spite of the beautiful weather, I'm surprised to find it challenging to ride around town. It is hard to stop and go on the hills. I have to use both hands and both feet to carefully synchronize the release of the clutch, letting go of both brakes and pulling the throttle. If I make a mistake in my timing, the motorcycle will slide up or down the hill and I will lose control and drop it. The pavement is also slotted with streetcar tracks, and I have to maneuver constantly around them to avoid getting the front wheel jammed. After touring the city for a couple of hours, I end up in Haight-Ashbury. It's been fourteen years since the last time I was here, twenty-six years old, on my first trip outside of Israel. Back then, I had no idea that this country would become my home. That Gili and I would marry and move to New York. That we would be raising a family in the northern suburbs. That I would become a technology entrepreneur. That I would come back here on the back of a motorcycle.

At night in the motel, I sit down and write. Words roll out of my fingers in a downpour of keyboard strokes, filling the white screen with black virtual matter and mirroring my voice back to me. I read the words back from the screen and realize that I have changed. At the beginning of my journey, I was isolated. I stood in the pouring rain of wisdom and just let it slide over my surface, never allowing it to penetrate the shell. The crises, doubts, and challenges then slowly gnawed holes in me, allowing some of that rain to settle. Slowly, I've become porous, like an absorbing sponge. In the remaining two weeks, I will be meeting with experts who can flood me with their wisdom. I am now ready to take it all in and then finally go back home.

Day 25, October 13th:
Meeting with Dr. Phil Zimbardo

PHIL ZIMBARDO GREW UP IN THE SOUTH BRONX GHETTO IN NEW York City. As an adolescent, he observed people exhibiting compassionate and heroic behavior within the crime, scarcity, and violence that surrounded them, and he became fascinated with human nature. Years later, as a young professor at Stanford University, Zimbardo conducted the seminal Stanford Prison Experiment — providing us with one of the most striking mirrors of human behavior, evil and good, and the factors that affect it. In the experiment, students were randomly assigned to play the role of either a prisoner or a prison guard in a simulated prison that was established in the university basement. They were given instructions about the role they were supposed to play and reminded that, at any point, they could ask to be removed from the experiment and return home. Within a few days, the students who were assigned the roles of guards started to exhibit violent behavior toward their fellow students, who were assigned the roles of prisoners. Those "prisoners" could have opted to leave the experiment, but instead, they continued to tolerate the abusive behavior of their peers. As the experiment continued, the level of abuse increased, and eventually, it had to be stopped. Observing the behavior of the participants, it was clear that it was dictated mostly by the prison setting rather than their individual personality traits. But while most people conformed, not everyone did. A small number of students did not accept the rules of the prison and stood up against them. Zimbardo calls this minority of people heroes, the ones who go against the flow in situations where most people turn to violence and oppression. Today, forty years later, Phil Zimbardo is recognized as one of the most prominent individuals who shaped the face of modern psychology. He still studies the characteristics of evil behavior and of the heroes who stand against it.

We met in his San Francisco home, a few blocks away from my motel. Before asking him questions about midlife and the process of transformation, I was curious to learn more about his personal background, and how it became a driving force in his professional life.

I grew up in the ghetto in the South Bronx in New York. And if you grow up in the inner city, regardless of your background, your race, or your religion, you are surrounded by evil: by drugs, by corruption, by gangs, by prostitution. And the temptation is always there, because it is always easy money. And evil is fascinating, evil is different, evil is strange. The devil is more interesting to most people than God, because the devil is wily. And that's why, in fact, in psychology, there's a huge body of research that can really be fit on the evil: antisocial, and aggression, and violence, and there's very little research on heroism. Actually, there's very little research on good and a lot on the bad.

My orientation is that people are born with this incredible brain that gives rise to an even more incredible mind that gives us the potential to do anything that is imaginable. So we have the mental template, good and evil, that makes some of us caring and others indifferent, makes some of us creative other ones destructive, and it pushes some of us to be villains: to do bad things for much of our life. But that same mind does the opposite: it pushes some of us to be heroes, putting our best selves forward in service of humanity.

My orientation, coming from this background in New York, was that I had friends who were good kids, who had gone bad, and even as a little kid, before I even thought about being a psychologist, I wondered what went wrong. And I wanted to believe that it was not something in them. I wanted to believe that if the situation were changed, they wouldn't have done the bad things.

"How important is the environment where you grow up? In what ways does it affect people?"

If you grow up rich, if you grow up privileged, you look around and you see success. Your father has a great job, etc., and you want to believe it's in your genes. So I think poor people, immigrants, minority people, in general, are situationists,[23] because it's the only thing that makes sense. You say, "If the situation would change, things will be better for us."

When I became a psychologist, I transformed this childhood orientation into becoming what's called a "situationist," that is to say, clearly, all of psychology is about the scientific study of the behavior of individuals. This is what all of the clinical psychology, personality psychology, cognitive psychology, neuro-psychology — all of them about the person. And, of course, the people are the actors on the stage of life, but — you're never alone. There are always other actors, it depends on how you dress, it depends on what role you are playing, it depends on who's doing the stagecraft, it depends on the props. So, essentially, social psychologists like me say, "Hey — of course we look at what the person brings into any situation, genes matter, personality matters, your habits matter, your response tendency, but — that's not enough to understand and enable me to predict your behavior. I have to know what the social context is in which we're going to place you and observe your behavior — give you a chance to be good or evil.

"What was your first reaction to the Stanford Prison Experiment? What were the immediate insights that surfaced and surprised you?"

That was really a unique demonstration, almost like a Greek play: what happens when you put good people in a bad place. Does the goodness of the people dominate and change the bad place, or does an evil place corrupt good people. The evil place was a simulated prison in the basement of the psychology department at Stanford. People asked, "Why don't you just go study prison?" Well, there the problem is confounded: you have bad people; many of the prisoners are bad people, and some of the guards are failures in the police department and military. So there you have a mix of the good and bad people populating it, in a bad environment. And the sad conclusion of the Stanford prison study, which is the same conclusion as Stanley Milgram's line obedience authority,[24] is that situations dominate in ways that we never fully appreciate.

That it's the majority of people who succumb. You put good apples in a bad barrel, you know what — the barrel wins. You take a sweet cucumber and you put it in a vinegar barrel, it becomes a pickle, no choice.

But the key is, it's the majority, in the Milgram experiments, two-thirds of people go all the way, shocking an innocent person, and in the Stanford prison study, most of the guards were cruel and abusive. However, in all those situations, there's always a small number of people who resist, defy unjust authority. And we can consider those people heroes. Not simply that they don't go along, but they go to the next step and challenge unjust authority, defy corrupt systems. And that's the kind of thing I am studying now: what is it about some people that enables them to resist the tremendous pressure of the situation and rise above it to act heroically?

I ask Zimbardo about going on the road: "If certain situations dictate a certain behavior and a certain mindset, does being on the road put you in a situation that lends itself to become a transformative experience?"

Most of us arrange our lives so that every day is like yesterday. If you have the ability, the resources, to lead a secure, stable life, where there are no daily challenges, you do, which means you know nothing about yourself. That is your comfort zone. When you purposely put yourself in a totally new situation, like getting on a motorcycle and riding across the country, every day is different. In that situation, you are constantly adjusting to something new, constantly out of your comfort zone, and that's the point at which you learn who you are.

Many of the experiments in social psychology, like the
Stanford Prison Experiment and the Milgram experiments,
put people in *new* situations. College students have never
been prison guards. So in that new situation, they try to
rely on what they've learned in the past, but it's not working.
So what's interesting about those studies is the character
transformation under the intense pressure of the moment.

The Milgram study is fifty minutes; the Stanford
Experiment is day after day, but it's every guard shift.
Prisoners have to adjust: now what do I do with these
three new guards? Once you adjust to those three, there
are another three guards, who are coming on the night
shift... So essentially, what these experiments do is, it
forces people to get out of their comfort zone and live
on the edge.

"So, being on the road is a new experience, and pushes you
to the edge, but is it important to literally be on the road,
moving from one place to another?"

In previous years, among people who could afford it, when
you graduated, you went abroad. You went to a new place,
a strange place, you visited foreign countries. And this was
partly to get you out of your comfort zone, to be where
not everybody speaks your language, and people have
different customs. Now, more and more college students,
even those who are not rich and privileged, do travel. And
essentially, travel (as you did — riding across the country
on your motorcycle) forces you to say: "who am I?" in a
totally new culture and place. This is why, for many people,
travel is one of the most important aspects of becoming
an educated person. Traveling out of your comfort zone.

"If you decide to travel for this purpose of leaving your comfort zone and putting yourself in entirely new situations, is it necessary to go on your own?"

It's key to travel alone. When you're with somebody else, everybody treats you as a couple and they don't intervene, and then, in fact, you spend your time with the other person and you are really not attentive to the environment around you. So, it's critical to travel alone, and most people fear that. If you want to understand yourself and the world around you — do it alone.

Zimbardo has studied a process called "dehumanization," where a person becomes easily prepared to attack another person (or group of people) by demonizing the other party, not thinking of him or her as human. While I was on the road, I started noticing people more; seeing people for what they are, rather than a job or a function that they fulfill. I think of this process as the opposite one — "humanization," where you realize that others you meet are as human as you are, and they experience a similar range of emotions and thoughts in their inner world, just by virtue of being human. I ask him if this process of "humanization" is something that has been studied before.

Dehumanization is the central process of all prejudice and discrimination. You take an individual and you treat him or her as part of a category (based on religion, race, origin, etc.) and then all of the stereotypes of the category are dumped on that individual. It's a filter that prevents me from knowing the real you, it prevents me from humanizing you. And in the extreme, I treat you like an object, and in the more extreme, as not comparable: you are not similar to me, my kind, or my kin. I put you in another category as "the other." The danger in dehumanization is that I treat you as less than human. In 1994, the Hutu government in Rwanda goes on the radio and says, "Your neighbors the Tutsi, whom you've lived with for decades, are nothing more than cockroaches. Imagine that your house is flooded with cockroaches — what do you do? We're going to have to kill them. So we're going to give every man a machete and every woman a club; your job is to get rid of the cockroaches." It was the most explicit attribution of dehumanization: your neighbors that you have lived with and whose kids went to school with your kids are cockroaches. And in 100 days, they killed 800,000 Tutsis. The weapons of mass destruction: a machete and a club. And once the killing started, it became more and more cruel. It was rape; it was beheadings.

This is what I call the hostile imagination. It's a term created by Sam Keen, a social philosopher in California: before going to war, every country uses propaganda that dehumanizes and demonizes the enemy, so that the citizens will hate the others and will want their children to go and kill them. So the enemy is both hated and feared and then you have to destroy them. And it's such a terrible thing because it seeps into the culture in so many ways.

There's an important study that was done by Albert Bandura, my colleague at Stanford, an experimental study of dehumanization. Very simply put, a group of students from one college are supposed to train a group of students from another college on how to solve business problems. They are in separate rooms and don't see each other. When they get the problem right, you reward them; when they get it wrong, you shock them with a shock box — the whole group. So it's like the Milgram study only it's a group against a group rather than individuals. There are three groups in the experiment. Before the study begins, the assistant who takes the names of all of the participants goes into the control room and says that we are ready to begin. To the first experimental group, he says, "The students from the other school are here; we are ready to begin." To the second group, he says, "The students from the other school are here. They seem to me like animals" (dehumanizing), and to the third group he says, "The students from the other school are here. They seem to me like nice guys" (humanizing). It turns out that over the ten trials, for the neutral group, the shocks stay at the same level; for the dehumanized group, the level of shocks goes consistently up, systematically accelerating, and for the humanized group ("nice guys"), they shock the least.

"How does the opposite process (humanization) work?"

To humanize somebody is to give them an identity. It's to see what about you is like me. I created an organization called "The Heroic Imagination Project" and one of the assignments that we give people is, "You're going to start on a heroic journey by doing little things each day, none of which are heroic, but they are practicing the social habits of heroism. Heroes are people who sacrifice on behalf of others. Take a risk. Put yourself out for people who are suffering or to defend a moral cause, and be aware that there's some cost. To have a "big hero opportunity," you need a holocaust, you need earthquakes, some terrible thing. But to be an *everyday hero* (an ordinary person who steps up to the opportunity when it comes, who is preparing him or herself for a big opportunity), each day, do a small heroic thing; make somebody feel special. Start with the person who serves you in the cafeteria. First of all, notice the color of his or her eyes. I asked my Stanford students — I will give you $100 if you bet $50 that you know the name and eye color of the person who served you breakfast this morning. In a class of three hundred students, not a single one knew. My point is — you are dehumanizing people you interact with each day. Not negatively, but you're taking their identity away and seeing them as functionaries.

Or, as an everyday hero, your job is: Give one compliment a day to a stranger. The first thing that is going to happen: they're going to smile. And you are going to make their day. You can tell your mother that dinner was great or notice the earrings of the person who serves you or that they changed their hairstyle. And compliment people for things they said in a conversation: "I liked what you just said, it's going to make me think about it more." The compliment has to be justified; you can't fabricate. And you know what — it pays forward. That other person is likely to give someone else a compliment that day (and *you* feel better as well so it's really "win win").

The next step is: after the compliment, you enter into conversation. I say: "Gee, that's a great suit." And then: "I have always admired the way you dress, where do you buy your clothes." And now, I have a conversation.

You want to go from a simple compliment to engaging another person in conversation. This is true for your barber, the person in the cafeteria, the bus driver. These are people whose job it is to serve you, but apart from that role, they are people. This is how you recognize the humanity in all people that you meet, everywhere. And if we all did that, that's transformative. It's a skill that can only be perfected with practice — you have got to do it every day.

Compliments are rare in our society. I meet students who tell me twenty years later, "Your course changed my life." All of us had teachers who are inspiring (formal and informal). Put an anonymous note in the teacher's mailbox. They will not know who it is, so you are not buttering them up.

Phil Zimbardo's wisdom:

- Sometimes, behavior is dictated by situations where there's little free choice. If you want to change, find ways to be in situations that can drive this change
- Go on the road, alone
- Happiness comes from the love of mankind, "humanizing" each person you meet, and understanding that they experience life just like you do
- When you are in a situation that dictates violent or oppressive behavior for most people, you still have a choice to be a hero, to be among the minority of people who defy it

DAY 26, OCTOBER 14TH: CALIFORNIA DREAMING

THREE DAYS OF REST HAVE COME TO AN END, AND IT'S TIME TO GO back on the road. It is just now, after allowing my body to rest, that I feel the intensity and demand of the coast-to-coast ride: little aches have appeared, sore muscles, and random clicks in the bones. The motorcycle is in a similar state — showing a darker shade of oil on the dipstick in the morning. We are both ready to go home, but there's more work to be done to reap the benefits of this journey. After loading up the motorcycle, I walk to the reception desk to check out and take one last apple from the jar. The receptionist looks at me with surprise and says, "Are you leaving, friend?" Her question is odd and should not make any sense. We are not friends, and she knows that I am scheduled to leave today, so it's no surprise. Yet, in this situation, it somehow adds up. The people you meet on the road always have a special meaning. We may not see each other again, but for a brief moment, we are friends. I walk back to the motorcycle, fire up the engine, turn on the music, swing my leg over the seat, and take off. It feels good to be on the road again.

Later that night, at the Palo Alto Super 8, I sit at the desk to write and process the day. It was just riding. Nothing more. Riding through

Pacifica, through the woods in the valleys, through the California highways; a peaceful ride that smelled like the salty air of the Pacific Ocean. A reminder of the unperceivable fact that I am actually here, on the West Coast.

Day 27, October 15th: Conference at Stanford University Led by the Dalai Lama — Scientific Explorations of Compassion and Altruism

When I was planning the *RIDE*, a friend told me about the Scientific Explorations conference, taking place around the same time that I would be in the Bay Area. The timing and location were ideal. I would near the end of my journey, already absorbed with my insights, and would have the opportunity to attend a rare meeting of the minds with the Dalai Lama and with leading researchers who study the science of inner peace. Arriving in Palo Alto yesterday, I was full of hopes and expectations of learning something new, and this morning, after 45 minutes of circling to find parking, I am now finally in Memorial Hall, waiting for the conference to start.

The opening panel includes Phil Zimbardo, and I am curious to hear him discuss his lifelong work again. As the day goes by, I am surprised to discover that brain surgeons, psychologists, and neuroscientists work jointly with Buddhist monks on the study of compassion and inner peace. The discussions converge Buddhism and modern-day science in a very natural way. But beyond the fascinating research that is presented here, I am excited to see a group of people from different backgrounds who are joint by their values; to see a movement that strives to transform humanity from the inside out. I have not realized it so far, but I am already a part of this movement. In the past few years, I adopted their mission in my professional life. Now, it has also become my personal mission. I want to use what I've learned to help others change their lives: to help others go on the road.

Day 28-29, October 16th-17th: Inner Peace between Palo Alto to Los Angeles

IN THE WEEKS THAT WENT BY, TIME GRADUALLY SLOWED DOWN, and now, it has come to a complete halt. Towns fly by and the weather changes, but the buzz of the miles remains still. The motorcycle goes down the Pacific Coast Highway in a steady pace, riding down the slopes of Big Sur, over the bridges, and into the woods, immersed in the salty smell of the ocean. The hours are loaded with new experiences, and at the same time, nothing happens. Song after song plays on the speakers, but inside, there is quiet. Acceptance. Love for everything that there is. Happiness without smiles. Emptiness of the good kind. This is it. What I was looking for. Inner peace. I count down the days until I go back, but home feels more distant than ever. It keeps sliding away as I ride toward it. I try to imagine the flight back and I can't. In the reality that was formed in the past few weeks, it seems impossible.

On Sunday afternoon, I arrive in the outskirts of Los Angeles on Interstate 5. It is rainy and chilly. The grey pavement stands below a dome of grey sky, supporting a row of cars stuck in typical LA traffic.

The Southern California palm trees shake in the wind, confused by the unusual weather. On the speakers, Guns and Roses' "Paradise City" is playing in full volume. Axl[25] screams to the California air, asking to go *"where the grass is green and the girls are pretty,"* asking to go home.

DAY 30, OCTOBER 18TH: MIDLIFE MEN AND A WORD OF ADVICE TO WOMEN

ACCORDING TO JAMIE PENNEBAKER, THE BENEFITS OF WRITING come from putting mental/internal experience (feelings, thoughts, and emotions) into the structure of language. This is precisely the challenge for men. Instead of words, men often communicate using rituals of action. In his book, "*Travels with Charley — in search of America*," John Steinbeck provides a faithful description of such actions: "*For I have always lived violently, drunk hugely, eaten too much or not at all, slept around the clock or missed two nights of sleeping, worked too hard and too long in glory, or slobbed for a time in utter laziness. I've lifted, pulled, chopped, climbed, made love with joy and taken my hangovers as a consequence, not as a punishment. I did not want to surrender fierceness for a small gain in yardage. My wife married a man; I saw no reason she should inherit a baby.*"

When a man goes through the challenges of midlife, he seeks the actions that will replenish the strengths that he had as a young man — to become a "mensch" again — inside and out. My experience during the past month on the road was a lot like Steinbeck's "lifting, pulling, and chopping". There was a lot of strapping, tightening, leaning, checking, and cleaning.

Men are often compared to children, and when they reach midlife, they are said to "buy themselves a toy." This saying may be accurate, but there are different types of toys. As a parent, when I buy toys for my children, I try to get "educational toys." My humble advice to women whose partner is a man of a certain age is this: Encourage him to get a quality toy that comes with a variety of positive activities. Polishing, fixing, greasing, and riding are your man's way of sharing his feelings.

Day 31, October 19th: Meeting with Byron Katie — Who Would You Be Without Your Story?

BYRON KATIE AND I MET FOR THE FIRST TIME IN ONE OF HER workshops at the Omega Center, in upstate New York. I had known of her and of her work but had not seen her before. Her personality and the sheer power of her presence left me with a strong impression. She was empathetic and kind, but at the same time unperturbed by strong displays of emotion. Guiding but not dictating. Humorous and respectful at the same time. Today, we meet again at the Crowne Plaza hotel in Los Angeles, where Katie is teaching the School for The Work to more than three hundred students. I finish setting up the lighting and cameras, and when she walks into the room, I immediately sense the powerful, pleasant presence that I remembered from our meeting in New York.

I first ask her about midlife and about the typical midlife patterns she identifies in the people she works with.

Here's a story about a man who was always surrounded by young, beautiful women. Now he's getting old and

going through a midlife crisis and these women look like little girls to him and they're no longer attracted to him. He suddenly sees the beauty and richness of the older women he meets. So the story he was believing ("I am only attracted to young, beautiful women") wasn't true. He is attracted to older women as well, and he didn't realize that. Now, after this realization, he sees that midlife is an opportunity to experience new kinds of relationships. He has changed, and the stressful thoughts that he used to believe are no longer true for him. The fourth question of The Work—"Who would you be without your story?"—is very powerful when you question a thought that you have believed for most of your life.

"Many people feel like they want to introduce change in their lives, but they are not sure how to go about it. What do you suggest?"

My experience has been that no human being has more wisdom than another. As we experience these questions that I call The Work, we're able to tap into the wisdom that we all have. The answers that arise when we question our stressful thoughts can transform our lives. All the spiritual texts talk about the what; The Work gives us the *how*. When you start questioning what you believe it expands the mind; the mind is free to be creative rather than stuck. And in that creativity, there's no problem we can't solve. For example, you can step out of your life and get on a bike and ride across the country. You've found freedom from the thought "I can't."

"Can you explain the concept of "loving what is"? How does it get one individual and groups of people to be at peace?"

"Loving what is" isn't a concept; it's an experience. It's more than simply accepting reality; it's loving it with all your heart, and anyone who uses The Work as a daily practice will eventually fall into the space where everything in the world is perfect, just as it is. Some of us are waking up to this; everything in its time. No one's ahead, no one's behind. It's like a flower opening. All it takes is a little water, a little sunshine, a little kindness.

"Loving what is" is about wanting what I have rather than wanting what I don't have. If I want what I don't have, when I get it, I'm still in the same position as before: I have that thing, but now I want something more. It's that carrot that we dangle in front of our eyes. When we don't understand what we have, we see ourselves as victims, and victims are violent people. But when we understand how the mind works, we're always delighted with what we have, and we realize that we don't need anything more. When we thoroughly question our stressful thoughts, what we're left with is gratitude and laughter.

KATIE'S WISDOM:

- Reality is always kinder than the story we superimpose onto it
- When you argue with reality, you lose – but only 100% of the time
- Everything happens for me, not to me

DAY 32, OCTOBER 20TH:
MEETING WITH DEEPAK CHOPRA —
THE BATTLE BETWEEN COLLECTIVE
CONSCIOUSNESS AND EGO

THE FOG IS STILL IN THE AIR AS I RIDE THE FINAL LEG OF THE TRIP, from Los Angeles down to San Diego. Slowly, the city tapers off into outskirts, the traffic loosens, and yellow hills with little Spanish houses appear at the side of the road. Inside of me, there is a quiet excitement, like a subtle smile that you can wear all day. An anticipation. These are the last days of the *Ride* and the first days of a new chapter of my life.

The Chopra Center is located within the La Costa resort, in the town of Carlsbad. By the time I arrive, the fog has turned into a thin drizzle, and the entire resort is submerged in a trickle of rain. I leave the motorcycle at the entrance, next to the valet, and run to the Chopra Center to tell them I am here. Deepak is working in his office and congratulates me on making it. I drag him out to the rain to take a picture next to the motorcycle. The last thing he wants to do right now is go out, but he identifies my teen-like enthusiasm and accommodates.

My first question to Deepak is about the importance of humility. In the past five weeks, I have experienced a strong sense of humility in the face of nature, the grandeur of the planet, and the kind heart of the people I met. Humility surfaced as a value, a compass for life, and a source of inner peace.

A few months ago, I went to Thailand to be ordained as a Buddhist monk, because I have been curious about it for almost twenty years. You know, you have these romantic ideas of giving up everything and disappearing into anonymity, and seeing what that experience is. So I've done that in different ways and forms. I've been to India at the Ashram of Sri Ramana Maharshi in Arunachala, where, on his 100th birth anniversary, we circumnavigated a mountain and there were a million of us, in silence. And in two to three hours, you become part of the ocean of humanity, like a drop in an ocean of water. And there is totally no sense of individuality, just "all of it." It was a really exhilarating experience. So I do these experiments to see if I can detach from my ego personality, so that was part of the reason to go to Thailand.

I went through the ordainment and lived the life: I slept on the floor; there was no mattress. There was no bed, clothing, there was no pillow, a few mosquitoes. We had to go on an alms-round carrying our begging bowls through the streets of the village and bring home whatever was given to us. You could never ask for anything; you only accepted what was graciously given. We had one meal; We stayed in silence, and from 2:00 a.m. to 6:00 a.m., we meditated first on the idea of impermanence and then on our own physical death. We visualized the death of the body, the cremation, and ultimately, the death of the mind. It was very valuable.

"Does some of it have to do with being fully present? It seems like the present moment always lends itself to humility, but the ego is focused on past and future accomplishments. How can one bring oneself back when the mind wanders and the present moment is lost?"

In Thailand, I got to experience the present moment as never before. When I left, the abbot said to me, "All of your spiritual learning is useless if it doesn't change your life. All the academic knowledge is useless if it doesn't change your life. And I will give you one piece of advice, which is probably the totality of our philosophy here:

> "The most important time in your life is now
> The most important person in your life is the
> one you're with now
> And the most important activity in your life is
> what you're doing now
> The rest is theory."

The past and the future are illusions. They exist in imagination. I think that the basic struggle of humanity is that they are trying to fix what can't be fixed. The change can't be fixed; it's a flux. You can't fix the flux, so you jump into it, you dance with it, you flow into it. It's the only way to live, actually, and I find that, for me, it's an increasing reality.

I ask Deepak about love. About the feeling that there is an invisible thread that connects everyone and everything. It seems like the more present and the more humble one is, the more this thread becomes visible. His response surprises me in its extremity: it's not that we are connected. We, as individuals, simply do not exist:

The individual doesn't really exist. It's a hallucination. There's no such thing as a person. That is a total hallucination. Every word you utter, every sentence you speak, every idea you have, is not your own (unless you have the most creative idea, like the Theory of Relativity, or you have a breakthrough in quantum physics. Even those ideas, by the way, are already part of the collective consciousness. They're gestating in collective consciousness) and they are "born" or delivered through a particular nervous system. But, in the end, there is only the universe recycling itself as a person.

So, everything you call "me" is actually the recycled universe. Your body is the recycling of the earth, the water, and the air. You're part of the single energy field that's everywhere, otherwise, how would you send email or surf the information highway on the Internet. The energy that is your body is not different from the energy field that is the universe. All your thoughts are recycled information; even your breath is recycled atmosphere. So there is no you. It's just an impermanent flux of the universe. The daily meaning of this realization is that there's freedom. There's nothing to defend and nothing to attack.

When I ask Deepak about the possible relationships between the fact that "there is no you" and daily positive practices like random acts of kindness, he says, "Different strokes for different folks."

For me, personally, the only thing that has value is insight. When you have the insight and you know it, there's nothing left to do. There is no practice. I've been there; I've written The Seven Spiritual Laws of Success, but I think there comes a stage where there is really nothing to do. It's all so clear and simple, that insight is like a mutation in consciousness and once that mutation occurs, there's no going back and there's nothing to do really, it's all taken care of.

There are different schools of thought. A lot of Buddhists will say that these practices help you realize the unity of existence. Vedanta would say: no — it's the other way around. When you recognize the unity of existence, these practices come spontaneously. Then, in fact, if you're trying too hard with these practices, you get stressed out because you are trying to do something that is not already a deeper insight or enlightenment.

I am confused. I tell Deepak about the experience of riding in heavy rain in Tennessee. The effort and the challenge were valuable to me. It made me proud to exert the effort and overcome the challenge. "Isn't it contradictory to step out of your comfort zone but also have things be effortless?"

The challenge is just a challenge in your mindset. Where I grew up in India, walking in the rain (for example) was considered romantic. People write songs about it. They go and dance in the rain; they like to get wet. And there are even festivals around it. If that's your mindset, then it's not a challenge.

When I was in Thailand, we used to go barefoot with the begging bowl. So there were no shoes and you had to step over pebbles and rocks and streets and shrubs, and I was not used to it, and it was tough for me. When I came back, the first day, the abbot asked me if it was difficult for me. And I said — yes, "Yes, it was very painful". He said, "You know, it's painful when you put the foot down but the other foot you lift, that has the absence of pain, which is very pleasurable. Just put your attention on that foot." And the next day, I did that and the pain was gone.

So — it's where you put your attention. It's all interpretation.

If you go out of your comfort zone with the whole mindset of embracing uncertainty and stepping into the unknown, then you've already shifted before you arrive.

It seems like the ultimate goal is, therefore, to go out of comfort as a means of *expanding* your comfort zone, getting comfortable with what's outside. The uncertainty that Deepak talks about is simply life itself, and the "comfort" of the comfort zone is an illusion.

"Do you need to possess inner strength to go on the road and feel that it is effortless?"

I've never used the word strength in my vocabulary. I used the word flexibility (in consciousness). In fact, I have a favorite saying that comes from the Yoga Vasistha, "Infinite flexibility is the secret of immortality." It's, in a way, an evolutionary principle that you adapt. It's not the strong who survive, but the ones who adapt. An oak tree is very strong but with the first storm, it may crack, whereas a little thin vine that is flexible will survive the same storm. So, I think more in terms of flexibility. Flexibility is an attitude more than anything else. It means that I don't need to always be rigidly attached to anything: a situation, a relationship, a point of view, or an outcome. If you are flexible, the challenge is gone.

DEEPAK'S WISDOM:

- Humility is a key to happiness
- Humility can be more easily achieved when the mind is present-focused
- People as individual entities are models of the mind. In reality, all is one, and love comes naturally
- Once you're out of your comfort zone, the effort is gone, and you experience life
- Flexibility is the very source of inner strength: "Infinite flexibility is the secret of immortality"

In the evening, I go back to my room at the resort. I unpack and sit down to write. It is getting late, but a rush of adrenaline keeps me awake. In two days, I will see Gili, Dana, Tomer, and Ori. In two days, I will finally be home.

Day 33, October 21st: Meeting with Sonja Lyubomirsky — on Happiness, Ways to Achieve it, and Chasing Your Dreams

IN RUSSIAN, *LYUBOMIRSKY* MEANS "PEACE AND LOVE," AN APPROPRIATE last name for one of the world's leading positive psychologists. Sonja's debut book, *The How of Happiness*, was the first book to provide a set of science-based happiness strategies that were experimentally tested to work. At the start of her career, in her doctoral thesis, she studied social comparisons and how they affect people's moods and longer-term happiness. She found that unhappy people tend to focus on their neighbors' grass instead of their own good fortune.

We meet at Sonja's office at the University of California in Riverside, a ninety minute ride from Carlsbad, through constant drizzle. My first question to her is about happiness and money. What is the relationship between the two? I know some studies show that in general "money does not buy happiness" but it surely can't be that simple.

There are hundreds of studies on money and happiness. Money makes people happy — if they spend it right. Of course, money can make you happy because money can allow you to quit your horrible job and write a novel, if that's what you really want to do. It can allow you to spend more time with your friends and travel to fascinating destinations. If you spend it on brand-name designer products and lots of material things, that is not going to make you happy. Unfortunately, that is what a lot of people do with money; they just "buy more stuff."

The correlation between income and happiness is positive but is much higher if you are poor. If you are poor, money definitely makes you happy. Past a certain point, if you already are okay, comfortable, it doesn't make a huge difference.

Here are some money spending tips:

- Spend your money on experiences rather than possessions (vacation, dinner with friends, not a bigger TV)
- Spread it on a lot of little things instead of buying one big thing (because we adapt). Take five smaller trips and not one huge one
- Don't get into debt — that makes you really unhappy
- Spend money on others rather than on yourself

Money also improves your health, amazingly, even at the very high levels. Someone who makes $600,000 a year is distinctively healthier than someone who makes $300,000. It is not clear what the reasons are. It could be social status, respect, and prestige, making you healthier. It could be that you simply can fly to Europe to get the better treatment.

"What about status and ego or self-importance? That often comes with the accumulation of assets. Is it detrimental to a person's happiness or mental health?"

Money also gives you social status and respect, and that is actually something people *don't* adapt to. So, unlike the kick from chocolate, sex, or a new TV, the "kick" from being important to others does not go away. This actually means that social status is a good thing, because it does not tend to be addictive (like things to which we adapt quickly).

"So, this seems like the difference between pride and vanity. Perhaps it's good to be proud and be important to others but not so good to be vain and self-important or constantly to be chasing a higher level of social status."

Social comparisons are definitely detrimental to your happiness. If you compare yourself too much — you can never be more powerful, or richer, or more successful than everyone else. There's always someone better off than you. If you get caught in the cycle of comparing yourself, no matter what social status you have, you want more. But that is external. You may have a very small ego but others give you some level of respect and without realizing it, it improves your well-being. The ego issue is different; it comes from within. One of my students, Joe, is planning to do a bunch of studies on humility. First of all, it's hard to measure it (self-reports are not reliable — if you say that you're humble, that is not a humble statement to make). One way to induce humility is to expose someone to something that makes them feel in awe. Something that makes them feel small by comparison. It could be a work of art; it could be the stars, some magnificent place in nature. But there is very little literature on this topic.

"Many of the exercises that you develop and test in your lab are "bottom up," meaning that they are daily "pedestrian" exercises, not related directly to changing perspective or making substantial life changes. What do you think about the opposite approach of "starting at the top" and trying to change things more fundamentally first?"

Interestingly, the two approaches completely converge! I actually get this a lot that almost everything I talk about, that almost everything that has been found by research to be effective has been written about in the bible or the scriptures of other cultures. The major difference between the two approaches is that the "top-down" approach (like institutional religion) is not designed to make people happy. The aim of religion is not to make people happy. I think it does — people are happier when they are spiritual or religious, but there's an overlap and it converges. But not everything.

The bottom-up approach is easy to follow and could lead over time to a significant shift. For example, there's research showing that if you want someone to like you, you should ask them to do you a favor. The idea is that once you help someone, you like them more (because you're justifying the help you've given — they must be a good person). That's a very bottom-up approach — almost like a trick.

"What is your take on the importance of being present and mindful? It seems like that is a fundamental ingredient in most transformative experiences. I feel like it's been a skill that I developed on my journey."

The past is important too (for example, Jamie Pennebaker's work about dealing with issues of the past through writing), and the future is also important (goals and a sense of purpose). There has to be a balance. The problem with the way most people live their lives today is that they are preoccupied with worry about the future and obsess too much about the past, so they need a "higher dosage of present" in their lives — to learn again the skills of savoring and mindfulness, skills we had naturally as children but lost along the way. In Western culture, we are losing life in the present. We're not so past-oriented but usually it's about the future: "Oh — I have to do this tomorrow..." but the present is all we really ever have. If we don't enjoy or savor the present, or be absorbed and engaged in the present, then what's the point of living? It's not good to always be in "what comes next" instead of now. "Is this interview helping me achieve my goals? And if not — it's a waste of time."

Phil Zimbardo found that homeless people were the most present-oriented people. And it's very functional — if you're homeless, you live day to day, but it's not good for the rest of us. We need to plan, we need to have goals, not just for practical reasons but also for the big, meaningful things in life: do you want to raise your children to be good, healthy, moral, happy people? Do you want to contribute something to the world? You can't just do that by focusing only on the moment. Bill Gates can't just focus on the moment; he has to plan ahead — who is he going to give the money to. And the past — there's definitely value in reminiscing about the past; remembering people who have passed away is important, so it seems like the obvious answer but there needs to be a balance.

I ask Sonja about taking risks, being adventurous, and leaving one's comfort zone. Is this one of the values for people who seek to live a more meaningful life? Do we need to teach our children to be more daring (while compromising some of their safety)? Is there something overly safe in our culture?

It's funny, I'm from Russia, and my parents travel back a lot, and when they come back, they always say, "Oh, America is so boring." And it's because everything is so easy; you drive to the Safeway, you park, and you get all of you groceries, and they're all there and all beautiful. And they're not even that expensive, and you put them in your car and you drive home. And over there, it's a huge challenge. Not only do you have to go to ten different stores to get what you need, and then half of them are out of what you want, but you also might get mugged on the way there. There's mafia everywhere. They say it's a "high" to be there. As parents, it's gotten extreme how risk-averse we raise our children to be: you don't let your kids make mistakes. My daughter just started walking to school in sixth grade. There are cultures where kids walk to school at age five. And still, my parents were worried: she's walking for two blocks by herself, she's going to get mugged, and she's going to get abducted on the way to school.

Research on regret shows that people are more likely to regret what they didn't do than what they've tried and failed at. And there are lots of reasons for that: when you didn't pursue that dream, when you didn't ask that girl out. You could have been humiliated, and you could have failed, but when you are humiliated and fail, you get over it pretty quickly, and you may also learn a lesson from it. Whereas, if you never try, you never fully get over it. What you really regret is the things that you didn't do.

Sonja's wisdom:

- Money makes you happy if you:
  - Spend it on others
  - Use it to experience new things
  - And have enough of it so you can make a living without having to borrow
- Small daily changes, or daily exercises, can lead to a profound change in life over time
- It's okay to be proud and seek external recognition for your accomplishments, but it could be detrimental to be self-important
- Love what is and avoid the comparisons to others or to what could be

- Reminisce on the past, plan and be optimistic for the future, but always keep your focus on this very moment
- The desire for safety can shut the door to experiencing life in full. Trying things (and allowing yourself to make mistakes) is a key part of your happiness

I thank Sonja, pack up the equipment and go back to the motorcycle. The ride back to Carlsbad is a rainy mess, catching me completely off guard, getting drenched in rainwater and stuck in traffic. With the last interview done and one more night to go before seeing my wife and kids, a cover of weariness falls on me. I am drained and homesick. Near Temecula, I stop at a gas station to get some coffee and stand under the small overhang of the convenience store to smoke a cigarette. People are flying in and out of the store in the rain, and the motorcycle is covered in shiny pearls of water. The rain will not stop. Then, on the other side of the door, I notice a woman in blue scrubs lighting a cigarette. She is standing right next to a stack of propane tanks. I point my finger to the tanks with a worried face and say "I don't think you should be smoking next to these tanks here." She smiles, takes a few steps away and says, "You think so?" It's funny how interaction with other people changes everything. Her smile shifts things back and my gloom is lifted. I put the cigarette out, wipe the seat with a rag, and ride back in the rain, all happy and excited to be home soon.

Day 34, October 22nd:
Poway, CA — Going Home

LATE IN THE AFTERNOON, I DROP OFF THE MOTORCYCLE AT A trucking warehouse in Poway, give it a big kiss on the tank, and take off in a taxi to the airport. In an instant, I am no longer a biker, just a guy carrying a bunch of bags. I sit in the back of the taxi and think about my motorcycle. How I'll miss it during the time it will be on its way back, strapped in the back of a truck. It held my weight for thirty four days, sliced through the curves of the coast, climbed up and down 8,000 feet on snow-covered mountains, rolled proudly through the desert, and charged on grated bridges and loose gravel like a war-hungry trooper. Never slipped, never broke down, and never asked for anything. What more can you ask for in a best friend?

It was exactly one year ago this week that I bought my first motorcycle, a tiny 250cc cruiser. I remember the day I went to pick it up. I turned on the engine, paddle-walked it to the edge of the parking lot, and for the first time, had to turn into live traffic. For long minutes, I stood there, anxious and sweaty, waiting for traffic to clear. Then, I finally gathered my courage and got on the road.

At the gate, the flight is delayed. I don't care. It took five weeks to get here, and it will take five hours to get back. Another hour will not make a difference. When everyone finally boards, it is well past mid-night, and most passengers immediately fall asleep. I cannot close my eyes. My heart is racing and my breath is short with excitement. I did it; I am safe, it is done, and I will be reunited with my family in only a few hours. At sunrise, I arrive in New York and sprint to the taxi line. When the driver hears my story, he steps on the gas and says, "Oh my. Let me get you home then!" The trees outside all wear the festive colors of fall. It's Saturday morning, and the world is calm, colorful, and embracing. Finally, we're home. It's 7:00 a.m. and everyone is sleeping. I open the door slowly, and the warm scents of home wrap around my entire body. I take off my shoes, close the front door, and go to the bedroom.

EPILOGUE

WE COULD NOT STOP HUGGING EACH OTHER ALL SATURDAY MORNING. Then, four days later, we drove down to a pet store in Queens and got a dog, a little Jack Russell that we named Daisy. In the weeks after my return, we spent the days closely together. Catching up and allowing the experience to sink in. We threw Tomer a big birthday party and together, taught Daisy new tricks. The time of year was magical, and the air smelled of new beginnings. Two weeks after my return, the truck came to our driveway and the motorcycle was back home, still dirty from that unexpected Southern California rain. The saddlebags were stuffed with cleaning spray and dirty rags and 5,793 miles worth of memories.

The *Ride* made me start a conversation with my future, older self. His advice is free of the fears that sometimes possess me, and his clarity of what's important to me in my life is astounding. I make it a point to have these conversations now, so that my dreams become his memories, instead of becoming his regrets.

The world changed. It's like watching a familiar movie on a High Definition screen for the first time. There are new details, colors, and sounds that were always there, but you hadn't noticed them before. Life is digitally remastered into a whole new experience, each and every day.

It is now time for the next adventure.

For videos, courses, and additional exclusive content, please visit:
www.rideofyourlife.com

RIDE OF YOUR LIFE

END NOTES

1. Adopting the term "intervention" from clinical psychology, positive psychologists often refer to activities and strategies to increase one's happiness as "positive interventions."
2. Caroline Miller's Second Book
3. An autobiographic novel published in 1963 describing Plath's clinical depression, later resulting in her suicide in 1971
4. A single-rider hovering vehicle used by storm troopers in Star Wars movies
5. A Harley Davidson motorcycle model, designed for long haul rides
6. A British Heavy Metal band that was active in the late 1970s and in the 1980s.
7. A minimal type of motorcycle helmet, covering only the top of the person's head
8. A large toy store in New York City
9. The Goldwing is a family of Honda motorcycle models that are designed for long haul ride
10. People often refer to cruiser-style motorcycle not made in the US as "metric" bikes, because the displacement of their engines is measured in cubic centimeters instead of cubic inches.
11. A chain of supermarkets
12. A hand gesture that US motorcyclists use to indicate the camaraderie of riding

13. Creole Townhouses are iconic pieces of the architecture of New Orleans' French Quarter. They are typically two stories high and have a large wrought-iron balcony on the second floor, facing the street.
14. The first track on Creedence Clearwater Revival's second album, "Bayou Country", released in 1968
15. An American motorcycle made by Harley Davidson
16. A song by Led Zeppelin lead singer Robert Plant, released in 1983, describing driving across the country as a way of life.
17. The Restaurant at the End of the Universe is the second book in the Hitchhiker's Guide to the Galaxy science fiction series by author Douglas Adams.
18. A 1966 Italian epic Spaghetti western film directed by Sergio Leone
19. An early type of electronic digital display with seven-line segments, showing the number eight when lit at the same time.
20. A 700-word ancient Hindu scripture
21. An American luxury automobile brand made between 1899 and 1958
22. Three-wheeled vehicles with two wheels in the front and one in the back
23. Situationism is the approach in psychology that attributes human behavior to the surrounding environment and circum- stances rather than to individual traits.
24. Interestingly, both Zimbardo and Milgram were classmates at the same high school in the South Bronx.
25. Axl Rose, the band's lead singer

MORE GREAT READS
FROM BOOKTROPE

My Fluorescent God by Joe Guppy (Memoir) In 1979, 23-year-old Joe Guppy was struggling with a bad breakup, but a few stomach pills drove him into paranoid psychosis… and straight into a mental ward. This raw, often comic memoir is a powerful spiritual and psychological adventure.

The Y'NEVANO Book of Encouragements by Wali Collins (Non-Fiction) Everyone has dreams, goals, and desires, but the challenges of life often get in the way. Y'NEVANO® offers more than 50 encouragements for becoming the person you truly want to be and living a fulfilling, regretless life.

Suitcase Filled with Nails: Lessons Learned from Teaching Art in Kuwait by Yvonne Wakefield (Memoir) Leaving behind a secure life in the Pacific Northwest, Yvonne Wakefield finds both joy and struggle in teaching art to young women in Kuwait. A colorful, true, and riveting tale of living and coping in the Middle East.

Heart and Sole: How 26 Ran Their First Marathon (And You Can, Too) by Melinda Hinson Neely (Non-Fiction) Heart and Sole is THE source of inspiration and practical information for anyone aspiring to run a marathon, a 26.2 mile journey that will change your life.

Discover more books and learn about our
new approach to publishing at **www.booktrope.com**.

26713563R00117

Made in the USA
Middletown, DE
05 December 2015